PALMER CEMETERY

and the

HISTORIC

BURIAL GROUNDS *of*

KENSINGTON &FISHTOWN

Vault stone and wooden sign. Mrs. James Sturgess is seen strolling with her son, James, and daughter, Rita Jo, on February 10, 1975. *Courtesy Urban Archives Temple University*.

PALMER CEMETERY
and the
HISTORIC
BURIAL GROUNDS *of*
KENSINGTON
&FISHTOWN

KENNETH W. MILANO
with the support of the Trustees of Palmer Cemetery

Charleston London

THE
History
PRESS

Published by The History Press
Charleston, SC 29403
www.historypress.net

Front cover, top image, photo by author.

Unless otherwise noted, all images are from the archive of Kenneth W. Milano.

First published 2011
Manufactured in the United States

ISBN 978.1.60949.242.7

Milano, Kenneth W.
Palmer Cemetery and the historic burial grounds of Kensington and Fishtown / Kenneth W. Milano.
p. cm.
Includes bibliographical references.
ISBN 978-1-60949-242-7
1. Palmer Cemetery (Philadelphia, Pa.)--History. 2. Cemeteries--Pennsylvania--Philadelphia--History. 3. Kensington (Philadelphia, Pa.)--History. 4. Fishtown (Philadelphia, Pa.)--History. 5. Philadelphia (Pa.)--History. 6. Kensington (Philadelphia, Pa.)--Buildings, structures, etc. 7. Fishtown (Philadelphia, Pa.)--Buildings, structures, etc. 8. Philadelphia (Pa.)--Buildings, structures, etc. I. Title.
F158.61.P25M55 2011
363.7'50974811--dc22
2010053700

Contents

Acknowledgements

This project would not have been possible without the cooperation of the trustees of Palmer Cemetery and Kensington Methodist Episcopal Church. I would like to thank Daniel Dailey and James D.B. Weiss for allowing me to work with the Palmer Cemetery archive, as well as Daniel Dailey and the other trustees at Kensington ME "Old Brick" Church for letting me search its archive, which was invaluable in gaining information and insight into the history of Hanover Street Burial Ground and the church's earlier cemetery.

My colleagues in Kensington and Fishtown history, Rich Remer and Torben Jenk, are present in everything I do, whether it is to borrow an image, ask a question or run an idea by them. I thank these men publicly.

Violet Lutz, Special Collections librarian at the German Society of Pennsylvania, deserves a special thank-you for the help she gave me while at that institution looking at the original 1765 register of Palmer Cemetery.

The entire staff at the Presbyterian Historical Society was very helpful when I was working there with the archive of the First Presbyterian Church of Kensington (plus they have free parking!).

A thank-you belongs to the staff members of Temple University's Urban Studies Center for allowing me to use several of its images in this book and especially to its archivist, John Pettit, who sent me images in a hurry.

I would also like to thank Walt Stock for the information that he provided to me on his Day and Hague family ancestry.

The nineteenth-century trustees of Palmer Cemetery deserve a thank-you, even though they are not around to hear it, for keeping such beautiful records, which are much fuller than those of their counterparts in the twentieth century, which is one reason this book is top-heavy on the earlier period.

I would finally like to thank my sons, Francesco and Salvatore, and especially my wife, Dorina, who put up with my finicky temperament near the end of pulling this project together (a week before Christmas 2010). As my wife's friend told her (her husband has written several books), a man at this stage of putting a book together is like a woman in labor.

Chapter 1
Anthony Palmer
Founder of Kensington

ANTHONY PALMER

The history of Palmer Cemetery (aka Kensington Burial Ground) starts with Kensington's founder, Anthony Palmer (1664–1749). Palmer was an English merchant who came to the Pennsylvania colony by way of Barbados as early as 1704. He had traded in Pennsylvania as early as the 1690s. Palmer first purchased several tracts of land in Pennsylvania from George Lillington. The entire tract, when combined, amounted to 582 acres. He added other acreage to his estate, calling it Hope Farm. This estate sat on the western bank of the Delaware River, about two miles north of the newly founded city of Philadelphia.

Anthony Palmer led an active life as a merchant, politician and landed gentleman. In 1709, he was invited to sit on the Pennsylvania colony's council. When Sir William Keith was appointed governor of the Pennsylvania colony in 1717, Palmer aligned himself with the new governor. Palmer's loyalty and patronage were immediately rewarded when he was nominated for the position of commissioner of peace for Philadelphia County the first year of Keith's governorship. Shortly after, he was appointed judge of the Court of Common Pleas and later in 1720 was nominated by Keith as one of the first masters of the Court of Chancery. Palmer's daughter, Thomasine, eventually married the governor's son, Alexander Keith, in 1731.

Because of Palmer's longevity (he lived to be eighty-five years old) and his time spent as a member of the council (he served on the council for forty years), he found himself the longest-ranking member of the council when James Logan, president of the council, retired in 1747. Palmer took Logan's place as president of the Provincial Council of Pennsylvania. As president of the council, Palmer became the acting governor of Pennsylvania on June 8, 1747, when Lieutenant Governor George Thomas left for England to care for his health. He remained acting governor until December 1748, when a new governor arrived from England.

Anthony Palmer married twice. By his first wife, Thomasine Dodd, he had a number of children over a long period of time. It has been estimated by the annalist John F. Watson that the Palmers had twenty-one children in all. However, only nine of Palmer's children have been identified, and only six of his children lived into adulthood. His three daughters who were born in Pennsylvania all lived long enough to marry. Three of Palmer's sons—Anthony, Francis and John—also lived long enough to marry. However, between the three sons only one male child lived to adulthood. This child, Samuel, the son of Francis, did not have any sons to pass on the Palmer surname.

Anthony Palmer's first wife, Thomasine, died in May 1745. She was buried at Christ Church, Philadelphia, on May 17. Even though Anthony Palmer was getting on in years, on August 13, 1748, at the age of eighty-four, he married twenty-year-old Catherine Allaire Carter, who was already a widow. Palmer, having outlived all of his children except Thomasine and Elizabeth, had hopes of having another child. No doubt Palmer would have liked to have had a son before he died, but no child ever came. He died the year after he married his twenty-year-old wife.

THE FOUNDING OF KENSINGTON

In early January 1730, Palmer purchased the Fairman Mansion estate from Robert Worthington. Along with the mansion house, the estate had a surrounding 191.5 acres. The Fairman Mansion property was located directly south of Palmer's Hope Farm property, on the Delaware River. The creek Gunnar's Run (today's Aramingo Avenue) was the dividing line between Hope Farm and the Fairman property. This new tract was situated northeast of the emerging district of Northern Liberties and southeast of Isaac Norris's Fairhill estate and Sepviva Plantation. Palmer sold Hope Farm to William Ball. Ball built a mansion near today's intersection of Richmond and Cumberland Streets, calling it Richmond Hall. This estate evolved into today's neighborhood of Port Richmond.

Anthony Palmer

With the purchasing of the Fairman estate, Palmer came into a property that was one of the more desirable and famous estates in the area. It was here in 1682 that William Penn first came to make the famous treaty with the Leni-Lenapes. The "Treaty Tree" was located about fifty feet east of the mansion, in today's Penn Treaty Park.

Palmer took up residence in the old Fairman Mansion, and in the 1730s he started to lay out streets and carve up the estate into variably sized lots. This real estate venture marked the beginnings of the town of Kensington. Like William Ball's Richmond, Palmer's town of Kensington was also named after a suburb of London. With the Philadelphia economy in a boom state during the 1730s, Palmer had no difficulty finding investors in his project.

Between the years 1724 and 1740, Pennsylvania experienced a rapid growth in population, as well as a tremendous increase in the economy. A large influx of German and Scotch-Irish immigrants marked this period. Many of these immigrants moved on into the interior to seek out a livelihood as farmers. With the rise of farmers in the hinterland, there was a corresponding rise for the need of shipping, shipbuilding and other related shipbuilding trades. The decade of the 1730s saw the shipbuilding production double in Philadelphia. As shipbuilders looked to expand their shipyards, they found that either the riverfront property was not available or Philadelphia's riverfront was too expensive. As Palmer laid out his lots in Kensington, its proximity to the city and its location on the Delaware River, with white sandy beaches, was quite inviting to the shipbuilding industry.

Once Palmer began selling lots in Kensington, a number of shipbuilders quickly invested. Shipwrights John Spencer, John Norris and James Parrock all invested in waterfront lots in Kensington. Ship joiners Nicholas Cassell and John George Ranseer also bought lots on the riverfront. By far the largest shipbuilder to invest in Kensington was Palmer's friend Charles West.

The fishermen families of George, John and Conrad Baker owned a combined riverfront frontage of 355 feet. This property was divided into four separate lots. The Baker family's properties were located slightly south of Vienna (Berks) Street and ran just northward of Otis (Susquehanna) Street.

When combined, the riverfront properties of those shipbuilders and fishermen accounted for almost all of the available riverfront property in Kensington (from today's Columbia Avenue to Dyott Street, or where the old Gunnar's Run Creek emptied into the river). These riverfront lots started on the east side of Queen (Richmond) Street and went eastward to the low-water mark of the Delaware River.

Between 1730, when Palmer first acquired the Fairman estate, and his death in 1749, he rented out more than fifty properties and sold more than thirty-five. Palmer's village of Kensington was growing, and the property values were rising.

SETTLING THE PALMER ESTATE

About the year 1745, Anthony Palmer began to think of setting up annuities for his wife and children. His health was poor, and he wanted to provide an income for his family when he was gone. By using a system of granting ground rents, he endowed his widow with an annuity of sixty pounds. His two surviving children were also given annuities of about forty pounds each through this same system.

Palmer died on June 2, 1749. He was buried at Christ Church Cemetery, Philadelphia. His estate, when settled on April 28, 1750, was valued at £2,341. The Fairman Mansion house was valued at £700. The value of the property lots still in Palmer's possession but that were not being rented was £1,641.

His estate was divided up among his heirs by giving Samuel Palmer, his grandson, one-fourth of the mansion house and three-eighths of the lots in Kensington. The total value of Samuel's inheritance was slightly more than £790. Elizabeth Allaire, Palmer's daughter, and her husband, Alexander Allaire, were left with one-half of the mansion house and two-eighths of the lots in Kensington, valued together at just over £760. Palmer's other daughter, Eleanor Berkeley, inherited one-quarter of the mansion house and three-eighths of the lots in Kensington, totaling about £793.

Samuel Palmer and Eleanor Berkeley gave their shares of the house to Elizabeth and Alexander Allaire, thus giving them the mansion house in full. Elizabeth had previously inherited the extra one-quarter share when her sister, Thomasine Keith, died before their father's will was executed. Samuel Palmer and Eleanor Berkeley were given extra ground lots to make up the difference in giving up their share of the house. With the house valued at £700, each quarter share was worth £175; thus, this money was replaced with the extra ground lots.

The number of ground lots in Kensington that were still in the estate's hands totaled over twenty lots. These lots made up 25 to 30 percent of the 191.5-acre district. The number of lots that were sold during the nine-year period of 1741 to 1749 amounted to roughly 50 percent of the land in Kensington.

Chapter 2
The Founding of
Palmer Cemetery

Palmer Cemetery on Early Surveys

While Anthony Palmer paid attention to making sure that his children and heirs were taken care of, he left out creating the deed of trust to found the Kensington Burial Ground (Palmer Cemetery). It is stated that it was his desire to set aside land for a community cemetery, but apparently he never got around to actually doing it. This task of creating a deed of trust would be passed down to his heirs.

While the Palmer estate was being settled, there were several surveys that were being made at that time (1750). A plot of land marked as "Anth. Palmer" in one survey shows the cemetery before it grew to its current size. Memphis Street (previously known as Lemon Street) was not cut through, and Cherry (Montgomery) Street, only thirty feet wide yet, went westward to a point that would be today's Memphis Street. At this point it became Mary Street.

The eastern half of today's cemetery was not yet part of the burial ground in the 1750s and had been given to Elizabeth Berkley, Palmer's granddaughter. This lot ran 380 feet on West (Belgrade) Street from Palmer Street to Cherry (Montgomery) Street and then went westward at right angles along Palmer and Cherry to a distance of 217 feet. This distance was almost exactly the one from today's Belgrade Street to the front gate of the cemetery that sits on Palmer Street. This is why the cemetery was shaped somewhat like a triangle on those early surveys, as the southern border on

Palmer Street was less than 9 feet long. Over time Elizabeth Berkley and her family sold off this lot, and eventually the trustees of Palmer would come to purchase it as two separate parcels from Christian Sheetz.

The cemetery was not exactly the shape of a triangle—rather it had the third point of the triangle (the northwest point) lopped off. One side, the eastern side, measured 380 feet (this bordered the previously described Elizabeth Berkley lot); the southern side (Palmer Street) was as mentioned not quite 9 feet long; and the western side (what would have been along the eastern side of today's Memphis Street) was 486 feet long. The northern side of the burial ground was not one straight line but rather ran 216 feet along Cherry Street westward from West Street before it made a forty-five-degree angle in a northwestern direction, running for about 71 feet before coming to join the western boundary.

Later on, after Memphis Street was cut through and Montgomery Street was widened (in the last quarter of the nineteenth century), a triangular piece of leftover land was created that sat at the cemetery's northwest corner. The trustees of Palmer purchased this lot and added it to the burial ground.

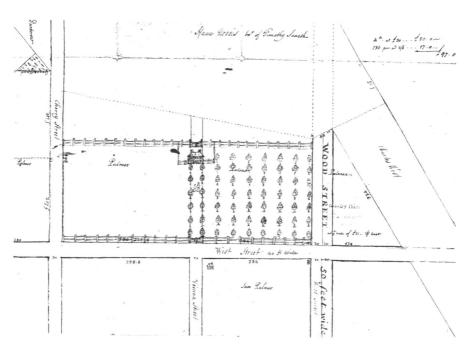

An early 1750s survey showing Palmer Cemetery (upper left-hand corner, labeled "Grave Yard"), a small fraction of its original size. Notice West (Belgrade) Street below.

The Founding of Palmer Cemetery

Fishermen's Hill along Memphis Street; the oldest section of the burial ground contains the remains of many members of the early fishermen families of Fishtown.

The cemetery land was not part of the lands that were divided up by the heirs of Palmer after his death—thus early on it was certainly being used as a burial ground, before the actual deed of trust was created in 1765. In one of the 1750s surveys, it is shown as a cemetery, with little crosses marked on it representing a burial ground. Thus, it is this westernmost piece of the cemetery—along the Memphis Street hill, where all of the old fishermen and shipwright families are buried—that is the oldest section of the present burial ground. This would make sense, since if you stand at the northwest corner of today's cemetery, it is easy to see that it is the most elevated section of the area. Having cemeteries on high ground was the normal thing to do, since flooding is the last thing you want to happen to your cemetery.

Lewis Evans's survey of the Palmer estate in 1750 was used in dividing up the Palmer lands. Evans started the survey in 1748 and finished in 1750. He showed the lot where the cemetery sits and labeled it "burying ground." This 1750 Evans survey, then, pushed the cemetery's founding back to at least 1748 or, most likely, earlier.

In the appendix of a pamphlet titled *A Plain Statement of the Proceedings Respecting the Kensington Burying Ground*, which was published in Philadelphia in 1817, it is recorded on the twelfth page: "The property which has given rise to the foregoing statement, is a burying ground, laid out about seventy years since, by Anthony Palmer, Esquire." Since the pamphlet was published in 1817, and it is stated that the cemetery was laid out "seventy years since," it is probable, then, that Palmer Cemetery was founded by 1747, or just before the death of Anthony Palmer, who died in 1749.

The only evidence that survives would thus place the founding of the cemetery in the late 1740s, although local lore has always had a wooden sign in the cemetery stating 1732 as the year of its founding. This wooden sign was constructed in the twentieth century. This 1732 year of founding comes with no evidence, except that Palmer started to lay out his town of Kensington in the early 1730s and thus perhaps laid out the lot for the cemetery as well. It's probable, but without any real documentation it could have just as easily been laid out later on.

ESTABLISHING THE DEED OF TRUST FOR THE KENSINGTON BURIAL GROUND

The establishment of the deed of trust that officially created the Kensington Burial Ground was made by an indenture of July 6, 1765. The grantors of the deed were Alexander Allaire, merchant, and his wife, Elizabeth; John Chevalier, merchant, and his wife, Elinor; and Samuel Palmer, gentleman—all of the city of Philadelphia, Philadelphia County. They granted the property to Emanuel Eyre, shipwright; Jehu Eyre, shipwright; Jacob Biderman, fisherman; Jacob Hill, fisherman; Nicholas Painter, cordwainer; and George Krouskop, house carpenter—all of Kensington, in the Northern Liberties Township of Philadelphia County.

The full deed reads as follows:

> *Whereas Anthony Palmer, late of Kensington aforesaid, Esq. the Father of the said Elizabeth Allaire, and the Grandfather of the said Elinor Chevalier and Samuel Palmer, being seized of a tract or Parcel of Land in the Northern Liberties aforesaid, did for the improving thereof, lay out and divide the same in convenient Town Lots, with several regular public Streets, Alleys and Lanes through the whole, which Town he was pleased*

to call Kensington, and is now so called and known by that name, And as an encouragement to the settlers of the said Town, did promise that he would grant and assure to them a Lot or piece of ground in Kensington aforesaid, hereafter to be described for a Public Burying Ground, to be freely occupied and enjoyed as such by all the Christian Inhabitants of Kensington aforesaid, be they what religion, condition, or denomination, whatsoever. And the said Anthony Palmer did leave open the Lot of Ground hereinafter described for the use aforesaid: And the same was used in his lifetime by his direction for and as a Public Burying Ground for all the Inhabitants. But he happened to die before any conveyance or grant of the said Lot of Ground was made.

And whereas Thomasine Keith, one of the Daughters and residuary Devisees named in the Last Will and Testament of the said Anthony Palmer, by her Last Will and Testament bearing date the twentieth day of September one thousand seven hundred and forty-nine, in consideration of her Fathers said promise for her part and share, did give and devise her portion of one Acre and a half for the said Burying Ground, and did desire her Executors to execute such Deeds as should be judged necessary for the confirmation thereof. (She the said Elizabeth Allaire, being at that time the only surviving Executrix,) named in the Last Will and Testament of the said Thomasine Keith—deceased.

And whereas a considerable number of the inhabitants of Kensington, belonging to either of the Protestant Churches, as well English, as German, have besought the said Alexander Allaire and Elizabeth his Wife, John Chevalier and Elinor his Wife, and Samuel Palmer, to annex to this Grant of a Burying Ground, the liberty to erect and build on the hereinafter describe Burying Ground Lot a School House; to teach children Reading and Writing, in the English and German Language, and to instruct them in the principles of the Christian Protestant Religion, used and professed by the inhabitants aforesaid.

Now this Indenture witnesseth, That the said Alexander Allaire and Elizabeth his Wife, John Chevalier and Elinor his Wife, and Samuel Palmer, in consideration of the premises, have given granted, and confirmed, and by these present do give, grant and confirm, unto the said Emanuel Eyre, Jehu Eyre, Jacob Biderman, Jacob Hill, Nicholas Painter and George Krouskop. All that Lot or piece of ground situated in Kensington aforesaid, Beginning at a corner of Orange Street, thence North thirty degrees East by Jacob Cooper and Henry Keppel's Lots, four hundred and thirty feet to *a post in the line of _____ Lot, thence by the same South fifty nine degrees East, one hundred and twenty feet to a post on the South West side of Cherry Street, thence by the said Street, South eighteen degrees East two hundred and ten feet to a post, thence by a Lot of the said John Chevalier and Elinor his Wife, South seventy-one degrees and a half West three hundred and eighty feet to Palmer Street, thence by the same North eighteen degrees West to the place of beginning; together with all the singular rights, members and appurtenances thereunto belonging.*

To have and to hold, the said Lot or piece of ground and premises, with the appurtenances unto the said Emanuel Eyre, Jehu Eyre, Jacob Biderman, Jacob Hill, Nicholas Painter and George Krouskop, their heirs and assigns for ever. Upon trust nevertheless to and for the several uses, intents and purposes hereinafter limited and declared and to, and for no other use, intent or purpose whatsoever; that is to say that they the said Emanuel Eyre, Jehu Eyre, Jacob Biderman, Jacob Hill, Nicholas Painter and George Krouskop, or a majority of them shall and do as soon as conveniently can be, regulate or cause to be regulated, the said hereby granted Lot of ground for Burying Ground in a decent order; with such Walks, Ornaments and Fencings as they shall think fit, or as the circumstance will admit of and shall from time to time, appoint a proper person who is inhabitant of Kensington, to be the Grave Digger of the said Kensington, and agree with him upon a fixed price for digging the Graves.

Which price is to be paid by next of kin or by the Executors or Administrators of the deceased, And the Grave Maker so appointed as aforesaid, shall dig the Graves in such order and agreeable to such regulations as shall be so made as aforesaid. And that no Christian person who at the time of his or her decease, shall be resident in that part of Kensington, which by the said Anthony Palmer deceased, was laid out for a Town or have any estate or interest therein, shall under and pretence whatsoever be refused his or her Burial on the hereby granted premises, (except a Felo de se) lawfully found so by the Oath or Affirmation of twelve men before the Coroner Supervisum Corporis.

And that the said Emanuel Eyre, Jehu Eyre, Jacob Biderman, Jacob Hill, Nicholas Painter and George Krouskop, their Heirs and Assigns and all and every such person and persons as shall succeed them, or either of them in the aforesaid Trust, shall suffer and permit such of the inhabitants of Kensington, as belong to any of the Protestant Churches to build a School House, on that part of the hereby granted Lot which is fronting on Palmer Street, whenever they the said inhabitants shall be able to raise money sufficient for building the same.

And that for this purpose such quantity of ground on the front of the said Palmer Street, shall be left out at the regulating of the said Burying Ground, as shall be thought sufficient for the building of such School House, which when so built and erected as aforesaid, together with the ground as shall be thereto belonging; shall be and remain to and for the use of such religious Society, or societies, as shall have built or erected the same—agreeable to an Act of Assembly of this Province, made in the 4th Year of King George the Second, entitled an Act for the enabling Religious Societies of Protestants within this Province, to purchase Lands for Burying Grounds, Churches, Houses for Worship, Schools, &c.

And that for continuing and perpetuating the said Trust for the uses aforesaid, they the said Emanuel Eyre, Jehu Eyre, Jacob Biderman, Jacob Hill, Nicholas Painter and George Krouskop, or the survivors of them, or a majority of such survivors, shall upon the decease or removal from

Internments were not to be made on the schoolhouse lot—rather, a school for teaching English and the German language was contemplated by founders of the cemetery.

Kensington of any of them, choose another inhabitant of the same place in the room and stead of such Trustee, or Trustees, as shall so die or remove as aforesaid; and so loties, quoties, from time to time when and as often any of the Trustees herein named or so chosen as aforesaid shall die or remove. Which Trustees when so chosen, shall have the same Authority and Trust, as if they and every of them were named in this Indenture.

And that they the said Trustees, shall keep fair Books and make entries therein as well of all Burials made on the said Burying Ground; as of their Orders and Regulations of the Burying Ground, and School House Ground and of the choice of Trustees in manner aforesaid.

With this stated deed of trust, Alexander Allaire (et al.) and Emanuel Eyre (et al.) signed and endorsed the indenture in 1765. It was witnessed by Peter Paris and Cornelius Barnes. The Allaires, Chevaliers and Samuel Palmer then presented the document to Isaac Jones, one of "his Majesty's Justices of the Peace," acknowledging that this indenture was their intention and that everyone was of age. Jones recorded "receiving" the indenture on August 14, 1765; however, the actual recording of the document did not take place until September 12, 1787, by the recording secretary, Mathew Irwin. The document was recorded in Deed Book No. 18, page 615.

Chapter 3

The Original Palmer Trustees and the Revolutionary War

THE SIX ORIGINAL TRUSTEES

The six men to whom the Palmer descendants granted the cemetery became the six original trustees of Palmer Cemetery. It is unclear how it fell to these particular six men to become the trustees. It may be a simple matter that these men were leaders in the community, or perhaps they might have even had a relationship to the Palmer family and thus the family knew and trusted them. The six men were all well known to Kensington as leaders in their respected business circles (shipbuilding and fishing) or as veterans of the American Revolutionary War.

The Eyre brothers (Jehu and Manuel) were leaders of the shipbuilding community and served as officers during the American Revolution. Their fishermen counterparts Jacob Biderman and Jacob Hill were members of a couple of the leading fishermen families (who were the reason for the "Fishtown" moniker). Shipbuilding and fishing were the two main industries in eighteenth-century Kensington. Why Nicholas Painter, a cordwainer (shoemaker), and George Krouskop, a house carpenter, were chosen is not clear—perhaps they were chosen to represent other sectors of the local economy or areas of the neighborhood. What is clear is that from the very beginning there was a heavy German influence in the history of the Kensington Burial Ground as four of the six original trustees were either German or had German backgrounds (Biderman, Hill, Painter and Krouskop).

Jehu Eyre (1738–1781) and Manuel Eyre (1735–1805) came to Philadelphia from Burlington with their brother Benjamin to learn the craft of shipbuilding under Richard Wright. Jehu and Manuel married two of Wright's daughters, Lydia and Martha.

All three Eyre brothers were veterans of the American Revolutionary War and had previously been commissioned by Washington to build naval vessels for the war. During the time the British occupied Philadelphia, they sacked the Eyre family shipyard, resulting in a total loss to the family of almost £6,400. The Eyres were never compensated for this loss.

Jehu Eyre's official military record reads that he was a captain in the Philadelphia City Guard in 1775; a colonel in the Philadelphia Artillery Battalion, 1775; and a captain of artillery, Philadelphia Brigade, under General John Cadwallader in 1777, serving at Trenton, Princeton, Germantown and Valley Forge; he later commanded the forts at Mud Island and Billingsport in 1780.

Jehu Eyre never quite recovered from an illness contracted during the war. He died of it in Philadelphia in 1781. He was buried at the old Coates Burial Ground in Northern Liberties but reinterred to a family vault at Laurel Hill Cemetery.

During the Revolutionary War, his brother Manuel became a colonel in the Continental army and a member of the Pennsylvania State Naval Board. He was a member of the Committee of Correspondence in 1775 and a delegate to the Provincial Convention of Pennsylvania, also in 1775. He was a private, later captain, in his brother Jehu's artillery, First Brigade, under General John Cadwallader in 1777, and he was also in the Philadelphia Militia.

Jacob Hill (circa 1738–1792) the Elder (to distinguish himself from his son and grandson of the same name) purchased a plot of ground on the riverfront in Kensington at Berks Street early on (1759). On August 8, 1772, he purchased a second lot nearby on the river. He was one of the early fishermen of Fishtown.

Jacob and his wife, Mary, had at least three children by 1760: Elizabeth, Mary and Jacob Jr. His daughter, Elizabeth, married John Rice, and his granddaughter, Catharine Rice, was the wife of Reverend George Chandler (1790–1860), the longtime pastor of First Presbyterian Church of Kensington.

The Original Palmer Trustees and the Revolutionary War

There is a Jacob Hill who shows up as a member of Captain Eyre's Company in the First Philadelphia Battalion of Militia for the Northern Liberties Township in 1776.

Jacob Hill Sr., the eldest son of Jacob and Mary Hill, was born sometime before 1760 and, like his father, was a fisherman. Also like his father, he became a trustee of Palmer Cemetery. Jacob Hill Sr. married a woman by the name of Elizabeth. She is the Elizabeth Hill who is the person responsible for the spread of yellow fever in 1793.

Hill family members are buried throughout Palmer Cemetery; one only has to walk a short distance to find Hill tombstones. They were in the neighborhood until well into the twentieth century and very well may have some members still living here. Many of them intermarried with the other prominent fisherman families of the day.

There is a Jacob Biderman (died circa 1776–79) listed on the muster roll of Captain John Hewson's Company of the Second Regiment of Foot. It was commanded by Benjamin G. Eyre, brother to Jehu and Manuel listed previously. Most, if not all, of the men in Hewson's company were from Kensington. Familiar names such as Christian Sheets (Sheetz) and Christian Fauns (Faunce) and Valentine Sorrick, as well as other fisherman family names as Baker, Pote, Gosser and more, all show that this was a Kensington-formed company led by Kensington's Revolutionary War hero, John Hewson, who was buried in Palmer Cemetery in 1821.

Jacob Biderman was selected as a trustee for Palmer Cemetery in 1765 and appointed to be a treasurer the following year. The earliest register of the minutes of the cemetery's trustees meeting has Jacob Biderman attending a trustees meeting on January 13, 1776, shortly after the start of the Revolutionary War. The first trustees meeting held after the British left Philadelphia in June 1778 was on February 2, 1782. At this meeting it is stated that Jacob Biderman had died.

On February 2, 1788, Jacob Biderman Sr. was selected to serve as a trustee of the cemetery. This is the son of Jacob Biderman, the original trustee. He is shown by at least 1802 as serving as the treasurer of the board of trustees, the same as had his father. Jacob Biderman Sr.'s estate was settled on February 13, 1816. Like his father, he was a fisherman of Kensington; his wife was named Catharine and his children were John, Henry, William, Samuel, Catharine, Mary and Jacob. This last child, Jacob Biderman Jr., would take the position of trustee after his father died, as had his father before him.

The grave of John Hewson (1744–1821) and his two wives. A renowned textile printer and Revolutionary War hero, he was a founder of the Kensington ME "Old Brick" Church.

Nicholas Painter (died between May 12, 1784, and May 7, 1787) appears on the 1769, 1774 and 1779 editions of the *Proprietary, Supply and State Tax List of the City and County of Philadelphia* for the Northern Liberties, East Part, which included Kensington. He was a cordwainer.

Painter is found in Captain John Hewson's Company, of the Second Regiment of Foot, commanded by Benjamin G. Eyre. As mentioned previously, this was a company formed mainly from Kensington. His will was written on May 12, 1784, and proved on Mary 7, 1787—thus he died between these years.

The final original trustee is George Krouskop (circa 1728–1783), who was born Johan George Krauskopf at Darmstadt in the Grand Duchy of Hess. His name has always been mangled in the paper records, where it is seen as "Krauskob," "Krausskopf" and "Krauskopf." In his will it is George Krouskop. He came to America in 1753 and became a member of

Zebiah Smallwood (died 1815), second wife to John Hewson. Her uncle, Captain Cheesman, died at the "Battle of Quebec" with General Montgomery. *Courtesy Todd Fielding*.

the German Reformed Church in Philadelphia. He married three times, his first two wives passing away very quickly; however, he had ten children with his third wife, Anna Margretha Wild.

Krouskop was generally identified as a carpenter and sometimes as a house carpenter. During the Revolution, there is a George Grosskup who appears serving duty as "Guard at the Goal" in October 1775. He also shows up as a member of Captain Eyre's Company in the First Philadelphia Battalion of Militia for the Northern Liberties Township in 1776. It is probably the same person.

One of Krouskop's daughters was Anna Maria (1764–1842). She married John Fulmer (circa 1763–1824) about 1785 in Philadelphia. John was the son of Michael and Catharine (Zoll) Vollmer. The couple started out residing on Palmer Street on land that Anna Maria was said to have inherited from her father. John Fulmer and his wife had several children, one a daughter named Sarah Fulmer (1793–1875) who married Johannes Widener (1790–1876). Sarah and Johannes's son was Peter Arrell Brown Widener (1834–1915). He was the famous Widener who became a transportation magnate, helped

John Fulmer, Catharine Day and their son, Andrew, uncle, aunt and cousin, respectively, to Peter A.B. Widener, one of the wealthiest men in American history.

organize U.S. Steel and the American Tobacco Company and, along with J.P. Morgan, was a top shareholder in International Merchant Marine, the owner of the White Star Line, whose flagship became the *Titanic*. Peter's son, George, and grandson, Harry, both died in the sinking of that ship. Peter A.B. Widener became one of the richest men in America's history. Widener's uncle, aunt and cousin are all buried at Palmer Cemetery.

THE KENSINGTON BURIAL GROUND'S FOUNDING YEARS

During the course of research to write this history of Palmer Cemetery, it was discovered that the oldest register of the Kensington Burial Ground's trustees meeting minutes still existed. Long out of the hands of the board of trustees, this early register was presumed lost to history. At some point in time, the register was donated to the German Society of Pennsylvania in Philadelphia. The name William S. Earley of 1322 East Berks Street is written on a note inside the register. This Earley is probably related to James Earley, who was a trustee at one point in the cemetery's history. He may have given it to the society due to the fact that the first seven pages of the register are written in the old German script handwriting. Earley may have never bothered to skip past these first seven pages to see that the register is in English thereafter. In any event, the cemetery's archive lost one of its prized possessions.

This register is dated from the first year of the creation of the deed of trust in 1765 and runs until March 1817, when the board of trustees became unstable due to several deaths. There are no recordings of meetings between 1817 and January 1833, when the board was resurrected. Two pages of entries for 1833 and 1838 finish this register.

As was already stated, the first seven pages are written in old German script, showing the early German influence on the burial ground. These entries, all for the first two years (1765–66), show payments to various people for work performed in readying the cemetery. The first English entries are for December 1766. Between 1766 and 1773, there is mention of the cash received for burials, but there are no figures of the amount of burials or any names of individuals who were buried in the cemetery. A typical entry might read: "By cash received of sundry people buried in burying ground." Jacob Biderman became the first treasurer of the cemetery and Isaac Will the first gravedigger.

The cemetery started in 1766 with a £4.0.6 (or 4 pounds, 0 shillings and 6 pence) balance from 1765 and had an income of £4.17.0 from burials and £1.10.7 in donations by the end of the year. In 1772, the total balance in the treasury of the cemetery was £29.16.11. The cemetery paid George "Crowscop" money toward work he performed for the cemetery and also spent money for tools and materials (spade, hoe, nails, boards, shovel and lock), as well as money to pay people to cut the grass. The trustees appear to have done some minor work on the cemetery, but nothing major was done before the Revolution. During the years 1773 and 1775, the cemetery took in £23.19.1 from burials. The year 1774 has the first entry for which the number of burials was actually mentioned: forty-eight. There was £5.14.0 taken in for these forty-eight burials. The cost for burials is also mentioned to be £0.2.0 for adults and £0.1.0 for children under fifteen.

All six of the original Palmer Cemetery trustees served in some capacity during the American Revolutionary War. Some had brief stints in the militia; others, like the Eyre brothers, were very much engaged for several years, serving in major campaigns and reaching the rank of colonel.

This intrusion of the Revolution on Palmer Cemetery is shown for the years 1776 to 1779, when there are no entries in the register. When the register starts again, George Krouskop is shown handing in £23.19.1, which was stated to be for three years' worth of receipts for burials (1777–79). The exact entry of the receipt of Krouskop's monies states: "By cash received of George Crowscup for sundry persons burying in the burial ground being three years. One year ye Enemy was in possession of Philadelphia."

This reference is to when the British captured Philadelphia and occupied it from late September 1777 to June 1778. At this time, the British built Redoubt No. 1 at Kensington, one of ten redoubts that were laid out as part of the fortification lines that ran along the northern side of the city of Philadelphia. With British soldiers encamping at Kensington and all six of the trustees of Palmer Cemetery serving in the patriotic cause, the business of the cemetery came to a halt, except for the actual burials.

After the British had left and the business of the cemetery was taken back up, there was a small amount of money that had been saved. Henry Oerey was given a bond of £15.0.0 by the trustees, payable with interest. For the seven-year period after the Revolutionary War (1781–87), there were at least 336 burials conducted at Palmer Cemetery, or an average of 2 per month. During this period, the trustees took in almost £63.0.0 in burial fees. Some of this money went to erecting a fence between the cemetery and Henry Keppel's property and for paying Phillip Sorick for constructing a path through the cemetery. Sorick was working at this time as the gravedigger for the cemetery (at least from 1784 to 1789). Nicholas Painter, one of the trustees, borrowed £20.0.0, to be paid back with interest. Painter was also paid £11.11.6 by the trustees to erect a fence of red cedar posts and cedar boards around the northeast corner of the cemetery.

The war had had its impact on the Kensington Burial Ground. Jehu Eyre, one of the original trustees, took sick during the war and never completely recovered. He died in 1781, the second of the original trustees to pass. Jacob Biderman had died previously sometime between 1776 and 1779—it is not clear if it was due to the war or not. Soon after Eyre died, three of the other original trustees died within a decade: George Krouskop in 1783, Nicholas Painter in 1787 and, a few years later, Jacob Hill in 1792, leaving Manuel Eyre as the only surviving original trustee.

Revolutionary War entry for December 31, 1779, showing receipts for burials at a time when "ye Enemy was in possession of Philadelphia." *Courtesy German Society of Pennsylvania.*

As the men died off, they were replaced by new trustees from Kensington. In 1782, Conrad Smith was added to the board to replace Jacob Biderman; in 1784, Peter Browne and Andrew Day replaced Jehu Eyre and George Krouskop. Peter Browne was a veteran of the Revolutionary War. His life is documented in another book by this author, *Hidden History of Kensington & Fishtown*. Andrew Day (1734–1805) was the anglicized name of Andreas Tag, the father of Kensington businessman and philanthropist Michael Day (1782–1864). Fishtown's Day Street is named for the family.

When Nicholas Painter died, he was replaced with Jacob Biderman, a son of the deceased Jacob Biderman. After Jacob Hill died in 1792, and Conrad Smith died soon after, they were replaced with George Eyre and Jacob Hill Sr. George Eyre is probably the son of Jehu Eyre, the original trustee. Jacob Hill Sr. is the son of the original trustee Jacob Hill, the Elder.

Manuel Eyre was the last living of the original trustees of the Kensington Burial Ground when yellow fever struck Philadelphia in 1793.

Chapter 4
The Yellow Fever Visits Palmer Cemetery

THE YELLOW FEVER IN 1793

The yellow fever has a storied history in Philadelphia. There were eleven outbreaks of the epidemic between 1780 and 1820, with none worse than the outbreak of 1793. The yellow fever was a virus with a three- to four-day incubation period. At first you get a fever and then muscle pain, particularly in the back, after which headaches, shivers and a loss of appetite would set in. Nausea and vomiting begin and the fever gets higher. After three or four days, some people improved and got better; however, a large percentage did not and instead entered a toxic phase, lasting about a day. The fever reappeared, affecting various systems in the body, and the person became jaundiced, hence the name "yellow fever." Abdominal pain and vomiting would start, and bleeding might occur from the mouth, nose and eyes. Once this happened, blood appeared in the vomit and feces, and kidney functions deteriorated. You died within fourteen days.

In the outbreak of 1793, yellow fever was said to have caused 4,044 deaths in Philadelphia. The Census of 1790 gave the population of Philadelphia at that time to be 28,522. If you include the populations of Northern Liberties Township and Southwark, the total population for the metropolitan area would have been about 44,000, which means that about 10 percent of the city was wiped out. Comparing that to the population of Philadelphia today, reported to be about 1.4 million people, it would be as if Philadelphia had more than 100,000 people dying in four months. The magnitude of dealing with such a scenario is mind-numbing.

The 1793 yellow fever started slowly in August with the death of 325 people. It then increased dramatically in September, killing 1,442 people, and then got worse in October, when 1,976 individuals died, before finally subsiding when the cold weather started to set in. In November, there were only 118 deaths.

In 1793, Northern Liberties Township reportedly had 543 deaths from the fever. Most, if not all, of these deaths were in today's Northern Liberties, Kensington and Fishtown neighborhoods, as the rest of the Northern Liberties Township was mostly unsettled.

From August to November 1793, there were at least 169 burials at Kensington's Palmer Cemetery, all attributed to the yellow fever. In a four-day period in September, there were 31 burials. In 1793, there were no churches in Kensington, and since many other cemeteries were attached to churches, many Kensingtonians who died from the fever were probably also buried at their church's burial ground as well.

The outbreak in Kensington was attributed to Elizabeth Hill, the wife of Jacob Hill Sr., one of the original fishermen of Fishtown and the son of the original trustee of Palmer Cemetery, Jacob Hill, the Elder. She is said to have contracted the disease when she was sailing near the infected wharves in Philadelphia. In all likelihood, she was probably transporting fish to sell at the fish market at Front and Market Streets, something many fishmonger wives of Fishtown's fishermen families so often did.

Mathew Carey wrote a book about the yellow fever that was published in Philadelphia in 1794 and entitled *A Short Account of the Malignant Fever, Lately Prevalent in Philadelphia*. The 169 adults and children who were buried at Kensington Burial Ground took place between August and November as follows: August 1793, 25 burials; September 1793, 82 burials; October 1793, 57 burials; and November 1793, 5 burials (an average monthly burial rate of 42 per month for this four-month period, compared to a normal rate of 4). The worst day was on September 23, 1793, when there were 9 burials at Palmer on the same day. It was a busy afternoon at the old cemetery.

A "diary," published as *The Diary or Loudon's Register* on November 23, 1793, stated that

> [an] *Extract of a letter from a gentleman of respectability in Philadelphia, dated Nov. 14…a disease more terrible and destructive has never appeared*

SEPTEMBER.

DAYS.	Christ Church.	St. Peter's.	St. Paul's.	First Presbyterian.	Second Presbyterian.	Third Presbyterian.	Associate Presby.	Reformed.	St. Mary's.	Trinity.	Friends.	Free Quakers.	German Lutherans.	German Calvinists.	Moravians.	Swedes.	Baptists.	Methodists.	Universalists.	Jews.	Kensington.	Potter's field.	Total.
1	1				2	1		1					4			1					2	5	17
2						2			2		5		3	1							1	4	18
3	1	1			3	1							2									3	11
4	3		1	1	2		2	1		2			4	3							2	2	23
5		4	1	1	1	1	1				1		2	3							1	5	20
6		2		1	2			2	1		1		5	1							2	7	24
7	1			1	1			1	1		2		3								1	7	18
8	2	1		1	4	2			2		3		4	4		2					1	16	42
9		1	2			1			1	3			7	1	1						1	13	32
10	3			1	1	1		2	3	1	6		5	1							1	4	29
11	2	1			1		1		1		2		3			1					3	8	23
12	1	2	6		1		1		2		3		8	2	2	1					2	10	33
13	1	1			1	1			3	1	7		8	2		1					1	10	37
14	2	1	2	3	3	1			4	4	4		5	2							2	15	18
15	4	2		1	1	3	1		5	1	10		9	1	1	1					2	14	56
16	4	2	1	2	3	1			4	3	10		12	7		1					3	15	57
17	1	1	1	1	4	2			5	2	7		21	7							3	24	61
18	3	4	1	2	4	2			6	2	7		10	4		2					3	19	64
19	4	2		2	3	2			4		5		9	5							2	23	51
20	3	1	1	1	2	2		2	3		9		7	1		3					5	27	57
21	3	3		1	2	1			6		6		8	2							4	21	57
22	6	1		2	3	1	1		1		6		7	6	1	1					7	33	76
23	1	3	2		4				5	2	7		8	6							9	21	58
24		5	2	4	4	2			9		8		12	4							8	38	96
25	4		2	4	4		2	6			15	5		3							7	35	47
26	2		1	3	1			1	1	5	6	5		1							1	25	52
27	3		1	1	2	1	4	1	6		14		6	5							2	14	60
28	1	1	1	1	1	1				2			4	5		3					2	29	51
29	4		3	2	2	3		1	4	1	10		7	3		1					2	14	57
30	4	1	2	1	3			6	1	8			4	6		3					2	22	63

Page from Matthew Carey's book on yellow fever showing burials for September 1793. The Palmer Cemetery column is next to last, before "Potter's Field."

among mankind; a smith who had 19 journeymen in his shop, of these 17 took the disease, and ten of them died—one other who had thirteen, all took the disease and died. A shipwright, at Kensington, buried 16 persons out of his own family.

Besides Elizabeth Hill, the fishmonger wife of Jacob Hill, there was Morris Goff, a Kensington shipwright, who also died. Susann Cramp, of the later shipbuilding family, also perished, among many other Kensingtonians.

There were so many deaths occurring in Philadelphia that it is probable that Palmer Cemetery's trustees made exceptions for some of these burials and allowed people from outside of Kensington to be buried there, as it was necessary to bury the dead quickly.

THE YELLOW FEVER IN 1797, 1799 AND 1802

The yellow fever deaths in Kensington were recorded by Dr. Benjamin Rush, the noted physician. In a letter to Alexander Biddle, written on August 25, 1797, Rush mentioned that "four more [died] last night in Kensington." Another letter (September 18, 1793) from Rush to Biddle stated that "all [of] the Ross, the blacksmith family, died." Hugh Ross was a Kensington blacksmith who, besides his wife and child, also died.

According to R. LaRoche, who wrote a massive book *Yellow Fever*, published in 1854, the fever visited Kensington again, this time in 1797:

> *Very different was the extent of the prevalence of yellow fever in the year 1797. On this occasion, it once more assumed the character of an epidemic, less extensive and fatal, doubtless, than that of 1793 and some that followed, but of sufficient severity to merit a somewhat detailed notice…The disease prevailed about Pine Street wharf, Water and Penn Streets, and also, and principally, in the suburbs of Southwark and Kensington. While these spots were severely visited with the disease, the city, both along the wharves and at a distance from them, remained healthy from Walnut to Vine Streets. Some cases, it is true, occurred in the city proper in the course of September and October; but most of these were readily trace to the above sources.*

Dr. Rush again gave estimates of how many deaths occurred. This time his figure was over 1,200 deaths, broken down as follows: August 1797, 303; September 1797, 579; October 1797, 386; and September 1797, 24.

In this 1797 outbreak, Kensington was again hard hit. It was reported that Palmer Cemetery had at least sixty burials. Of these burials, a number were from early Kensington families with ties to the fishing and shipbuilding industries: Bakeoven, Baker, Bowers, Craemer, Sorrick and Sutton.

The introduction of the 1797 fever to Kensington was said by some to be due to communication with the ship *Hind*. John Bruster—of the Kensington family of Brewsters/Brusters who owned the Shackamaxon Street wharf—was one of the first to die. However, Bruster being the introducer of the disease was discounted by LaRoche as impossible, since witness Michael Lynn stated that Bruster never went aboard the ship and that he was ill before the ship ever reached port.

In another outbreak, from August to October 1799, there were fourteen people buried in the cemetery due to yellow fever, followed by an 1802

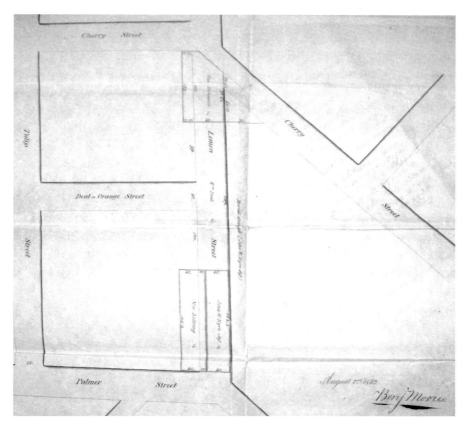

Survey showing the Everhard Bolton lot taken from Palmer Cemetery (Jehu W. Eyre and others) when Memphis (Lemon) Street opened in 1877. *Courtesy Philadelphia City Archives.*

outbreak during which forty-six adults and forty-nine children were buried at Palmer Cemetery. The year 1803 had yet another outbreak of the fever. According to a contemporary newspaper burial account (*United States Gazette*) of September 8, 1803, there were thirty-two adults and ten children buried at Palmer the previous month due to the fever. These various outbreaks of the fever took several notable Kensingtonians, including John MacPherson's wife and child (MacPherson's Square was his family estate); Alexander Allaire; three of the children of noted shipbuilder Francis Grice; and Jacob Miller, a Kensington shipwright.

Due to the yellow fever epidemic, the trustees felt it necessary to purchase adjacent lots to enlarge the cemetery before those lots were developed. On May 3, 1794, the trustees purchased from Everhard Bolton a lot measuring

40 feet by 166 feet, 8 inches that bordered the western side of the then smaller cemetery, land that today would be underneath Memphis Street. Then on March 19, 1796, the trustees purchased the first of two lots from Christian Sheetz, which bordered on the eastern side of the original cemetery. They paid $500 for this lot that measured 100 feet by 380 feet. Sheetz offered the trustees the second half of this lot, measuring 117 feet by 380 feet, for $1,200. This lot had three houses on it and sat adjacent to the east of the first lot they had purchased from him. This lot had West (Belgrade) Street as a western border and ran from Palmer to Cherry (Montgomery) Streets. The trustees purchased this second lot a couple of years later for slightly less than what Sheetz wanted. This double lot of Sheetz's was the original lot that Anthony Palmer had given to his granddaughter, Elizabeth Berkley. The Palmer family had sold it to Ebenezer Hazard and his wife, who in turn had sold it to Christian Sheetz in 1795, only a year before Sheetz sold it to the cemetery, making a profit along the way.

There were at least 377 burials at Palmer Cemetery due to the outbreaks of yellow fever between 1793 and 1803. During this same time, the Palmer Cemetery's trustees meeting minutes record 907 burials. This is 530 more burials recorded than was recorded as related to the fever. Looking at the average burials per month before the yellow fever came to Kensington, it shows that, spread out over the course of a year, the burials doubled due to the fever. The trustees spent their money wisely, as the size of the cemetery was doubled with the lots they purchased and they were able to handle the rise of burials.

Chapter 5
The Nineteenth-Century History of Palmer Cemetery

TIME OF EXPANSION AND LARGE TREASURY

Palmer Cemetery came out of the 1790s yellow fever epidemics in very good condition, financially speaking. The business of the cemetery, due to the many deaths, built up the treasury and allowed the trustees to expand the cemetery. With the purchase of the second lot from Christian Sheetz, the trustees came into possession of several houses that were located on the West (Belgrade) Street side of the property. At a meeting on June 19, 1802, a committee of Andrew Day and Jacob Biderman was formed to take charge of the houses and lots and rent them out to the best advantage of the cemetery and collect the rents. These rentals supplied the cemetery with another revenue source.

The next meeting that is recorded for the trustees was on January 10, 1806, almost three and a half years later. When they met in 1806, it was to appoint another trustee, as the last of the original trustees, Manuel Eyre, had died the previous year. Andrew Day had also died. These two positions were filled by John Coates Browne and Daniel Sheetz. John Coates Browne was the son of former trustee Peter Browne. He was a successful businessman and politician, a onetime president of the Kensington Board of Commissioners and on the board at the Kensington National Bank, among other things.

Before Andrew Day died, he had been the treasurer of the board. His son, Michael Day, who acted as the executor of his father's estate, attended

The tombstone of John C. Shibe (1754–1801), brother of baseball legend Benjamin Shibe's grandfather, whose family comprised part of the original fishermen families of Fishtown.

this 1806 meeting, handing in $752.46 for 382 burials. Some of the money his father had used to fence the cemetery and make repairs on the rental houses. Day's totals, combined with other reports from trustees, showed a total of 558 burials since the previous meeting.

Daniel Sheetz's tenure on the board of trustees did not last long; he had resigned by the next meeting on February 6, 1806. He was replaced with John Christ. The next meeting of the board did not take place until July 25, 1814, more than eight years later. Since that time, there had been at least 1,270 burials, an average of 84 burials a year, or 7 per month. The cemetery was under a new board of trustees that was already slacking off on its duty to convene from time to time. During these eight years that the board did not meet, members took in income from burials, rents and loans in the amount of $3,397.96. It was also during this time that accusations began to surface about the mismanagement of the cemetery. A large treasury with no board meetings can lead to these sorts of charges.

At the 1814 meeting, trustee John Christ had in his hands $918.21. He proposed that he "retain the sum he had in his hands" on "interest to give his judgment Bond...which was agreed." Christ's holding on to almost $1,000.00 of the cemetery's money would eventually cause him to be caught up in the first real crisis for the cemetery (recorded later here).

Both Jacob Hill and Jacob Biderman also offered to keep the money they had or smaller amounts of it on terms similar to Christ's, which was agreed upon. John C. Browne was appointed treasurer to manage the cemetery's money. Browne had previously invested some of the cemetery's money by buying stock in the Bank of Philadelphia. One final matter taken up at this meeting was to replace the deceased Peter Browne, the father of John C. Browne. Browne's place on the board was taken by Franklin Eyre, another of the family who had had at least five members serve on the board.

THE ATTEMPTED TAKEOVER OF PALMER CEMETERY BY FIRST PRESBYTERIAN CHURCH OF KENSINGTON

The second-oldest church in Kensington (after Kensington ME Church) was First Presbyterian Church of Kensington, founded in 1814. It was during First Presbyterian's founding that the controversy over Palmer Cemetery arose. The First Presbyterian Church was almost completely built by July 1814. Short of monies, one of the trustees of First Presbyterian, John Christ, informed the church that he could borrow money from the trustees of Palmer Cemetery, of which he was on the board.

As noted previously, Christ at this time was already holding $918.21 of the burial ground's money. He went to the recorder's office to view the deed of trust for the cemetery with another trustee of the church. He had been on the board of trustees of the cemetery for several years but had never read the deed of trust. After reading the deed, he realized that the board had been negligent in its duties. Christ approached the trustees to see about the church borrowing the money. The board did not want to loan the church money—since the money was already out on bond to Christ, the board suggested that Christ could loan the money in his name.

This conversation between the board members and Christ is not recorded in the trustees meeting minutes. For Christ, the arrangement proposal of the board for the loan to be in Christ's name was not to his liking. Christ was a newly converted Presbyterian, so perhaps he was beginning to doubt the viability of the church that he himself was helping to found. Soon after the board rejected the loan to First Presbyterian Church of Kensington, Christ resigned from his involvement in the First Presbyterian Church of Kensington. Whether he lost faith in the church or left in embarrassment in unknown.

In a pamphlet titled *A Plain Statement of the Proceedings Respecting the Kensington Burying Ground for the Two Year and Half Last Past* (Philadelphia, 1817) and published anonymously (Reverend George Chandler is said to have been the writer), it is stated that the burial ground had for the past two and a half years been mismanaged. According to the trustees minute meetings, there were no meetings in 1815 and 1816 during the time in question, so it is difficult to tell what happened during these years, but the descendants of the original board were certainly lax in meeting. With Christ out of the picture, the First Presbyterian Church congregation, led by its pastor George Chandler, became intrigued by the idea that the Palmer Cemetery Board of Trustees was not fulfilling its duties as prescribed by the deed of trust.

Certain inhabitants of Kensington, no doubt members of First Presbyterian Church of Kensington, thought that they might have a play to wrestle control of the cemetery from the trustees due to their neglect. This group, led by their pastor, sought out a descendant of Anthony Palmer's who might help them to take control of the cemetery. John David Schaffer was found living in Skippack Township, Montgomery County. A plan was devised that if Schaffer took the trustees to court and gained control over the cemetery due to their breach of the deed of trust, as established by his ancestor (Schaffer was the son of John Schafer, who married Elizabeth Chevalier, the granddaughter of Anthony Palmer), the trustees of First Presbyterian Church of Kensington would purchase the cemetery from him for $500, and the church would then follow the rules of the deed of trust.

While all of this sounded very altruistic, as if the church had the best thoughts of Kensington's residents at heart, it did not sit that well with the cemetery's board of trustees, an organization that was some sixty years old when this upstart church opened up shop in Kensington. While it was true that some of the infractions with which the cemetery's board of trustees was charged did exist, most folks in the neighborhood tended to overlook them, as they were minor and were things that had been going on since 1765, when the cemetery was officially founded.

The charges amounted to a trustee (George Eyre) being accused of not having lived in Kensington for some time, which was true, but he moved only across the street from the border of Kensington. Another accusation was that the trustees were burying people who did not reside nor hold property in Kensington (it was estimated that three-quarters of the burials that were taking place were not for people from Kensington). This also was true, but it was a practice that had been going on since the founding of the cemetery—for example, a child moved from the neighborhood after growing up, but when he died, he wanted to be buried with his parents at Palmer Cemetery. The final charge was the expense of exorbitant fees for burials that the trustees charged, stating that they needed the money for the upkeep of the cemetery. One witness was willing to state that the fence was built by subscription from the community. Another witness stated that it was known to the trustees that he had read the deed of trust and thus their family was not charged for burials but that others who had never read the deed were charged.

At first Schaffer was drawn into the conspiracy to wrestle control of the cemetery from the trustees. He delayed signing his name to any document because he wanted to receive a larger amount of money. First Presbyterian's people told him that he was actually due "nothing," since the land was actually deeded to the community as a cemetery. Also at this time, another heir of Anthony Palmer's was discovered, "Mr. Wagner, in Fourth Street." With this other heir found and squabbles present about the amount of money that should be paid, the plan started to become unraveled.

Schaffer had someone go to Kensington (he was staying at a hotel on Race Street) and talk with the current trustees. After investigations and an "unofficial" talk with a judge, Schaffer soon saw the folly of the plan and was advised by the judge that the case could not be won in any court in Pennsylvania. At this point, Mr. Wagner also dropped his interest in the case.

The First Presbyterian Church congregation tried once more to rally support to their side, calling a large meeting of inhabitants of Kensington at the schoolhouse behind their church (at this time the church was located on north side of Palmer Street, above Richmond Street). A committee went to see Mr. Wagner again. Wagner stated that he would take up their cause for $500 for the minors under his guardianship (the heirs of Anthony Palmer). The church committee balked and decided to drop the idea of getting heirs to fight for the takeover of the cemetery. Instead, the members decided to petition the state legislature for redress. Through misinformation, they were able to gather about ninety signatures.

The trustees of the cemetery did not take these attacks sitting down. They published their own pamphlet in 1817 titled *Candid and Just Statement of the Proceedings Relative to the Kensington Burial Ground: Of Its Actual Situation, and the Conduct of Its Trustees*. This pamphlet, with the signatures of the trustees of the cemetery (John C. Browne, George Eyre, Jacob Hill Sr., Jacob Biderman, Franklin Eyre and John Christ) and addressed to the "Inhabitants and Holders of Property in Kensington," charged that some of the trustees of First Presbyterian and their pastor had been slandering and spreading falsehoods about them. The trustees waited to publish this pamphlet until the state legislature heard First Presbyterian's petition, which they did before quickly rejecting it.

Now riding the high ground after receiving a winning decision from the state legislature, the cemetery's trustees had their turn at debasing the individuals involved in the attempt to take over the Kensington Burial Ground. They accused the First Presbyterian Church committee of trying all sorts of trickery to raid the cemetery's treasury to help pay off the church that they couldn't afford to build. This exchange of pamphlets resembles the pamphlet wars that were popular in the eighteenth and early nineteenth centuries.

The Kensington Burial Ground's trustees' pamphlet is a very witty response to Chandler's attack on them and included sworn statements by John Schaffer and Jacob Smith, the innkeeper of the establishment where Schaffer stayed and where conversations between Schaffer and Chandler took place. This tract helped balance the historical record of what actually occurred during this controversy that saw an attempt to take over the cemetery by First Presbyterian Church of Kensington. Thus ended the first recorded hostile takeover attempt in Kensington's history.

THE DECLINE AND REJUVENATION OF THE BOARD OF TRUSTEES

After the controversy subsided, the board of trustees got back to the business of running the cemetery. At the meeting of the trustees held on January 28, 1817, it was announced that Jacob Biderman Sr. had died. His position on the board was replaced through the appointment of his son, Jacob Biderman Jr., the third generation of Jacob Bidermans to serve on the board. Also in 1817, the old gravedigger Daniel Haines needed to be replaced—he was too infirm to perform his duties, plus he had moved out of Kensington. Frederick Hippensteel took Haines's place.

After the March 23, 1817 meeting of the board of trustees, there is silence in the trustees meeting ledger until January 5, 1833. These are the lost years, as there are no records of any kind. It's unclear what happened to cause a silence of almost sixteen years. It is possible that a volume of the trustees' minutes was lost, but the surviving records would seem to indicate that there is no missing volume of trustees minutes, as the original volume of trustees minutes stops at March 23, 1817; then, in the very same volume, it begins back up on January 5, 1833. This would seem to indicate that if there was a missing volume, it would have had to been kept separately from this original volume, since this original volume exists with the gap of years within it.

One possible scenario might be that a new secretary took over for the board of trustees and that he kept his own books. Once he passed, those books were not passed along, and the new incoming secretary, not having a register to work with, used the old one to start up again and record the meeting minutes since there was still room left in the original volume. However, this is not likely, because John C. Browne was the secretary at the last 1817 meeting, and when the records start back up again on January 5, 1833, there is a "Copy of a Receipt" in the original volume that states that the board of trustees has received from Peter Browne the "box which he says contains all the papers that his father John C. Browne had in his possession belonging to the said burying ground." This note is signed by Franklin Eyre. John C. Browne had been the secretary and treasurer of the board back in 1817. He died in 1832, and his son, Peter, passed along to the board the paperwork in his father's possession when he died, so he would appear to have held the position of secretary all those years between 1817 and 1832, when he died. We cannot be sure why the meeting minutes of the board of trustees between 1817 and 1833 were not included in this original volume, unless of course they were never kept to begin with.

The first trustees meeting recorded after this lull was dated January 17, 1833. At this meeting, Franklin Eyre appears to have been the secretary. It is mentioned that the deaths of John C. Browne (1832), Jacob Hill, George Eyre (1817) and Jacob Biderman had left four vacancies on the board. The four new men who were appointed as trustees were Peter Browne, the son of former trustee John C. Browne and grandson of trustee Peter Browne; Mathew Vandusen; Jehu W. Eyre, grandson of original trustee Jehu Eyre; and Frederick Emerick. John Christ was the other member along with Franklin Eyre. For some reason, Frederick Emerick's name is written but then crossed out—perhaps at this time he did not accept being a trustee. A new gravedigger was also appointed in Daniel Sheetz, who was to visit Frederick Hippensteel and procure the tools in his possession.

Mathew Vandusen's tenure on the board was halted when he resigned in November 1838. This is the last note in the original 1765 ledger of the trustees. A new trustees meeting minutes ledger was begun on January 23, 1839, with the following note by Jehu W. Eyre, who was only recently appointed as trustee in 1833, as the last surviving trustee:

The tombstone of shipbuilder
Matthew Vandusen, who was from
a family of prominent Kensington
shipbuilders. His family owned
Palmer's Fairman Mansion from
1795 to 1825.

*Whereas the Deed from the heirs of Anthony Palmer conveying the Kensington
Burial Ground in Trust to six persons, enjoins upon the survivors of them
the appointment of other Trustees to fill the vacancies that may occur—And
whereas Franklin Eyre one of the Trustees on the 21st Dec 1838 departed
this life—and John Christ and Matthew Van Dusen two others of the
Trustees resigned their trust and Peter Brown an other of the Trustees removed
to the city and was consequently disqualified to act. Therefore Jehu W. Eyre
the only remaining trustee, as soon as he could make a proper selection, did
on the 23 January 1839 appoint the following persons as his associates vis.
John Christ, above mentioned,—Frederick Emerick, Michael Faunce, Daniel
Dewire and Franklin B. Eyre. Kensington January 23rd, 1839. Jehu W.
Eyre, Surviving Trustee.*

With these words, Eyre reestablished the Palmer Cemetery Board of
Trustees. The board's resurrection would last for more than a hundred years
before declining somewhat again in the twentieth century.

The first meeting of the new board was held on February 9, 1839. It met
at the residence of Jehu W. Eyre, where the members appointed Eyre to be
the "Secretary and Treasurer." The books of the cemetery were pored over

by the trustees, and afterward it was decided to "procure an entire new set of books for the purpose of keeping the accounts, receipts, minutes"—thus these statements of Eyre initiate this new register for the trustees meetings. There is no mention at this time of keeping a register of individuals who were interred at the cemetery, only "accounts, receipts, minutes."

In 1839, Casper Herbell was invited back to remain as "gravedigger." The cost for burials at this time was $1.50 for those over twelve years of age without a case, $0.50 more with a case. For those between the ages of six and twelve, the cost was $1.00 plus $0.50 extra for a case, and for small children under six years of age, the cost was only $0.50, or $1.00 with a case.

The new board of trustees was very short on funds, having less than $4 on hand. This is a very different story from back in 1814, when it had almost $3,400 in the treasury. One has to wonder what happened to this money and whether the lack of records for the years between 1817 and 1833 has anything to do with it. The $3,400 in 1814 was a quite a substantial amount of money for that time. It would be equal today to about $43,000 if you used the Consumer Price Index as a guide or $600,000 if you were going by the Unskilled Wage Index.

After this initial meeting of the new board, the trustees did not meet again until five months later, in July 1839, and then again in December 1839. Much of their work was done in small committees, and the board did not meet regularly. During the July meeting, the issue of putting up wooden plank fencing along the Cherry (Montgomery) Street side using red cedar or oak posts was discussed. Due to the lack of funds, the trustees were forced to hew the posts themselves, hiring a day laborer to help put up the fencing.

It was known at this time that there would be a road coming through the western edge of the cemetery (Memphis Street), so they decided to have the western edge surveyed and put a fence up right along the western line as well so that when the street did come through, the fence would already be in place.

Also at this time, the trustees separated out from the cemetery a lot on Palmer Street adjacent to the cemetery that did not have internments in it yet—they wanted to rent it out to raise some funds. This property had previously been purchased from Everhard Bolton and sits under today's Memphis Street. The old fencing that had been taken down along Cherry Street was recycled and used for fencing around this Palmer Street lot, and they rented it out to Casper Herbell, the gravedigger, for his garden. Fencing was also constructed around the foot of the gardens of the rental houses along West (Belgrade) Street, separating them from the burial part of the graveyard. Also at this time, a walkway nine feet wide was laid out from West Street to the westernmost part of the original walkway that led from Palmer to Cherry Street.

Michael Faunce resigned in 1840 and was replaced by Frederick Rotan. In 1842, new rules were adopted to prevent fraud, which had been perpetrated on the trustees. From then on, an attending physician would have to note the residence of the deceased on the certificate; in the case of no physician, two neighbors would have to come forward as witnesses to the residence of the deceased when they died, and these had to be known to one of the trustees. A deed for the residence of the deceased could also be used to prove residency or ownership of property in Palmer's Burial Ground.

At the meeting of March 26, 1842, the trustees mourned the loss of one of their own, as John Christ had passed away on the fifteenth of the month. He was seventy-five years old and had been associated with the cemetery since 1806. George Auffort was chosen as the replacement for Christ based on a new strategy of the trustees to try and have the six trustees be spread out throughout the neighborhood so that at least one of them would know the future internments' neighbors. It was also mentioned at this meeting that the new rules they had enacted were too strict and causing problems. From then on, if the trustees knew you, you did not need any documentation of your residence. If you were unknown to the trustees, further proof from either the attending physician or property deed was needed. Help with clarifying these new rules was given by James Page. (Colonel James Page, an attorney, would play a role in suppressing the Kensington Riots two years later in May 1844.)

The First Presbyterian Church of Kensington in 1843 applied to the cemetery's trustees for permission to build a Sunday school on the lot of ground within the cemetery that was reserved in the deed of trust for a school. The trustees, after consulting with Page again, decided that the deed of trust gives the choice of *not* having a Sunday school on the property since at the time of the writing of the deed of trust the rise of the public school system was such that an "English & German Language School" was no longer necessary; besides, the building of a school would have interfered with the main gate to the cemetery on Palmer Street. The trustees rather wanted to keep the cemetery separated from any church denomination and refused the application.

At this point in the cemetery's history, the trustees were meeting either every six to twelve months. Occasionally, special meetings might be called to replace deceased trustees or decide other important matters. The meetings tended to be filled with reports from the "Fence Committee," which was always repairing and building new fencing, or with treasurers' reports, which detailed the

A view of the central carriage path looking toward the Montgomery Avenue gate. The oldest part of cemetery is located to the west (left) of this path.

money taken in from burials and the rental houses. Reports on the repairs of the rental properties—or other work done within the cemetery like cutting the grass, removing poison ivy, fixing sidewalks and more—were also reported on.

In 1846, Casper Herbell finally died and was temporarily replaced as gravedigger by Daniel Davis, who was replaced by John Myer as the permanent gravedigger. The trustees had all of the wooden fencing around the cemetery whitewashed at this time. This whitewashing was performed by Ann Herbell for $19.52. In 1848, the trustees had attorney James Page draw up a petition that they would present to the state legislature asking for exemption of paying taxes. Thomas Fernon, a local state legislator, was able to get tax exemption status for the cemetery. Fernon is the same man who had fought so hard in the mid-nineteenth century to create Penn Treaty Park but, at that time, failed. It was eventually built in 1893.

On June 6, 1848, George Auffort died. He was replaced on the board by Samuel Biderman, a member of the same Biderman family who had three generations of Jacob Bidermans serve in the eighteenth and early nineteenth centuries.

PALMER CEMETERY AT MID-CENTURY

When the year 1850 arrived, Palmer Cemetery was probably physically in better shape than it had been for a long time. The past ten years of solid stewardship had done a lot of good. There were major tree plantings along the outside of the cemetery, as well as inside; even though a number of the maple trees that they had purchased and planted had died, they were replanted a second time. Apparently the trees, bought at auction, were at the auction for two successive weeks, and the roots had been too exposed over this time. The trustees also had new brick sidewalks installed along Palmer Street, setting up the curbstone along the old line of the street, even though the district's plans were to expand Palmer Street by ten feet. By 1850, they had also put new curbing and paving on the West Street side of the cemetery. However, due to the deep digging they had to do for the laying of the pavement near the two upper rental houses on the ground, they undermined the homes and had to repair the foundations of the fronts of the houses, including adding high wooden stairs.

At the August 23, 1850 trustees meeting, the trustees were put in the difficult position of denying burial to a family who had a member commit suicide. While they felt for the family, the trustees claimed that they did not allow such cases to be buried at the cemetery.

September 16, 1851, saw the death of trustee Frederick Rotan. He drowned in the Delaware River. He was only fifty years old. To replace him on the board, Alexander Fountain was appointed.

The next meeting, in March 1851, was a special meeting called by the trustees due to some "impositions" placed on several of them. The board decided to make a new rule that required burial permits to have "the signature of two Trustees before the gravedigger could act on it."

At the July 29, 1851 regular trustees meeting, the news was announced that the cemetery would have to pay the District of Kensington $270 for the water pipes that were being laid along Palmer Street in front of the cemetery; soon pipes would also be laid along West Street that would cost the cemetery $380 more. It was also discussed that the District of Kensington was talking about bringing Lemon (Memphis) Street through, which would cause the trustees to lose the entire lot that they had purchased previously from Everhard Bolton. The trustees hired attorney Edward Waln to deal with the issue. Luckily, the trustees never used this lot for internments, so no removals would have been required. To add insult to injury, the District of

Kensington charged the cemetery for the water pipes that were laid in front of the lot that the district would be taking for Lemon Street.

With mounting debts, the trustees had to raise burial rates in 1851 by putting a $2.00 surcharge on each burial. The cost of burials now would be $4.00 for those fifteen years and older; $3.00 for those from seven to fifteen years of age; and $2.50 for those under seven years of age. At this time, Samuel Biderman moved to the Northern Liberties and was disqualified from acting as a trustee. He was replaced by Samuel Hussey.

At the meeting of September 14, 1854, it was announced that the twenty-eight maple trees that surrounded the cemetery were to be trimmed and a number of posts were to be put along the Cherry Street side of the cemetery to prevent carts from injuring the wooden fence. It was also ordered to acquire and plant maple trees along Palmer Street so as "to form an arch with those that are already on that front close in to the fence." The consolidation of Philadelphia County into the city was met with no fanfare in 1854. The cemetery now simply had to pay the city for the paving of Palmer Street and leftover water pipe bills.

It was at this time (1855) that a letter of application was received by the board of trustees from John Hulbert. Hulbert wanted to put an ornamental iron railing around the graves of his wife and mother-in-law. The application was debated among the board members, with only one in favor. The application was rejected. One reason given for the rejection was the following: "Although such enclosures might ornament cemeteries which are regularly and properly laid out, it would not apply to the Kensington Burial Ground and especially in the old part where their has been no order observed and where the graves interlock each other in numerous instances, rendering a multiplicity of such enclosures incompatible with a free passage through, over or about the Grave Yard." It was further stated that "[i]n the course of time the privilege might become so abused that vacant ground might be taken or fenced in, forming family plots, which would be contrary to the spirit of the trust."

In 1856, the City of Philadelphia laid water pipes along Cherry Street, charging the cemetery $326.36. Between these pipes, the ones on West Street and Palmer Street and the charges for paving half of Palmer Street, the trustees' treasury was raided by the government for the better part of the 1850s. The cemetery was finding it very difficult to build any sort of money up in its treasury. They had balances after paying debts hovering at about $10.00 or less for years, which required them to put off any major undertakings. On top of this, an arrangement that the trustees had with the city solicitor to pay in installments the debts owed the city was not carried over when a new solicitor took over in 1857. This new solicitor immediately had two writs drawn up against the cemetery, forcing the cemetery to pay the added expense of hiring a lawyer. The city was also charging the trustees for the entire length of paving along West Street, even though the new city plan after consolidation showed that Montgomery Avenue was going to be widened by twenty feet—thus there was paving on the cemetery's property on West Street that the trustees thought they shouldn't have had to pay since it was going to be taken away from them.

Having already raised the burial rates by $2.00, the trustees looked to the rental properties they had on the grounds for more income. The rents on all three houses were raised. Finally, on January 29, 1858, it was announced that the trustees had finally paid off their debts to the city. Also at this meeting it was announced that the city was making everyone place "house numbers" on their properties. The cemetery spent $0.60 to have tin numbers put up on the three rental properties along West Street. The cemetery, recognizing the horrible condition of the economy, proposed the increase of rents to be held until the economic depression was over.

During the July 28, 1859 meeting, the trustees, finally having their treasury in better shape than it had been for ten years, decided to have all three rental properties renovated. A carpenter, Jacob Murphy, examined all of the houses and recommended extensive work, which he carried out. The houses were in rather bad shape, and if they were renovated, the trustees could raise the rents. The Lower House, occupied by John Felty at this time, was in a very leaky condition. Rather than fix the roof of the shed kitchen, the trustees opted to have Samuel Hall, a carpenter, add an extension to the house and an extra floor above it.

When the January 30, 1860 trustees meeting was held, it was so ordered to create a "proper book for the purpose of registering the name, age and late residence of each person buried in the Kensington Burial Ground together with the date of the Permit for such burial; commencing at the date of the last meeting of the Trustees, which had been held back on July 28, 1859."

This "proper book" survives today as the first internment register for the cemetery's burials. The first burial recorded in this volume was on August 1, 1859. It was previously thought that perhaps the earlier internment volumes were lost, destroyed or burned up in a fire. However, through a close reading of the surviving records, including the original trustees meetings register at the German Society of Pennsylvania, there does not appear to be any trustees meeting ledgers or internment volumes missing from the cemetery's archive (besides the fact that the earliest volume is located at the German Society instead of the cemetery's archive). Instead, the missing years appear to have never been recorded. What is missing from the archive is most of the burial permits—small, loose sheets that were usually purchased from a printer in quantities of two thousand at a time. These slips were filled out by trustees for the family of the deceased and handed in by the family to the gravedigger for burial at the cemetery.

On January 30, 1860, there is the first talk of putting up an iron fence around the cemetery. A committee was formed to investigate it. There was one hundred feet of iron fencing installed in late 1860 along Palmer Street at a cost of $3.50 per running foot. It was started at the proposed Lemon (Memphis) Street at what today would be the entrance gate at Memphis and Palmer Streets and went eastward, halfway to Belgrade Street. A gate was installed at this time near the expected Lemon Street on Palmer, and attorney James Page was again hired to look after the cemetery's interest as it pertained to cutting through Lemon Street.

July 1860 saw a small controversy develop due to an error in an old land deed that showed one of the Emerick families owning land on the western side of West Street from Hanover (Columbia) up to Cherry (Montgomery) Street, which would have been part of the Christian Sheetz lot that now was part of the cemetery. Of course, the Emericks had never owned land between Palmer and Cherry along West Street; the deed actually had the correct measurement from Hanover up to Palmer but mistakenly called Palmer Street by the name of Cherry Street. This didn't stop an heir from demanding compensation from the trustees. However, he soon saw his mistake and it never came to court. This same July meeting noted the death of Samuel Hussey. His position as trustee was taken over by Conrad Baker, a member of an old Fishtown fishing family.

THE CIVIL WAR YEARS AND PALMER CEMETERY

At a trustees meeting held on January 29, 1862, the first mention of the Civil War appears in the meeting minutes. The war had broken out on April 12, 1861. At this January 29 meeting, Treasurer Jehu W. Eyre reported that:

There was due the Burial Ground from the tenant of the upper house on the 16th inst.—4 quarters rent amounting to $60 which she promised to pay or a considerable portion of it as soon as her son John Schwaab shall receive his wages as a soldier in U.S. Army for putting down the southern rebellion—there is some four or five months wages due him which he is looking for every day.

In some reports it is stated that perhaps upward of 1,300 men who served in the Civil War are buried at Palmer Cemetery. This would appear to be a fairly high number; however, since internment records do exist starting in August 1859, the task of seeing if this statement is correct can be achieved by a willing and able body. Certainly the reports of the trustees do not show any dramatic rise in burials—thus most of these Civil War soldiers were veterans, dying long after the war was over.

By the end of June 1862, the iron fence was completed along the entire Palmer Street side of the cemetery, and the trustees decided to repave that

Headstones belonging to the Eakins and Moser families. Christiana Moser was the wife of Samuel Eakins, commander of America's first submarine, the Civil War's *Alligator*.

side of the cemetery as well, in 1863. However, as the war was dragging on and the price of iron was rising, it was decided to abandon the idea of finishing the iron fence until conditions improved. Since they put off finishing the iron fence for a while, they built a new white picket fence between the West Street houses and gardens and the cemetery.

The year 1863 saw the trustees purchasing six blank books to be used by each trustee for burial permits. None of these books seems to have survived, but there are eighty-nine burial permits from 1865 and three from 1864.

At an October 4, 1864 meeting of the trustees, it was announced that longtime trustee Franklin B. Eyre had died. He was to be replaced by Joseph Paxson. Paxson would go on to serve on the board until he died in 1890, with many of those years acting as secretary and treasurer.

PALMER CEMETERY AT ONE HUNDRED YEARS OLD

While it was founded earlier, the cemetery was "officially" established by deed of trust in 1765 and celebrated its 100th anniversary at the time the Civil War came to a close. At the first meeting on January 29, 1866, after the Civil War was over, the trustees had an election, and Conrad Baker became president; Daniel Dwier, treasurer; and Joseph Paxson, secretary. This trio would remain in these positions together until 1877 and usher in a new era for the cemetery, filled with much-needed improvements and revenue sources for the cemetery. John Myer (or Mayer) continued as the gravedigger, a position he had held since about the 1840s and would continue to hold until 1873, when he died.

Since the war was now over and times were getting better, the trustees began building other portions of the iron fence. There was one hundred feet of fencing that went up on Belgrade Street. Metal prices, though, were still high, and the trustees paid almost two dollars more per foot than they did in 1860. Frederick Emerick, a longtime board member, resigned due to infirmity. He was replaced by Daniel Dwier's son, Daniel Dwier Jr.

At an 1866 meeting, it was necessary to call another person to the board— Jehu W. Eyre had died. Since the founding of the cemetery, there had always been an Eyre on the board. Jehu W. Eyre was replaced by Albert Emerick by a vote of three to one (Dwier wanted to elect another Eyre, Edward Eyre). Albert Emerick's nomination to the board in 1866 started a more than fifty-year period for his and his son's involvement with Palmer Cemetery; another Emerick, Frederick, had already served on Palmer's board.

Due to Eyre's death, the "Fire Proof" safe was moved from Mary Eyre's house to Daniel Dwier's—the $100 safe had been purchased by the trustees to keep the records of the cemetery. In 1867, the trustees had another seventy-five feet of iron fence put up along West Street, and the following year they completed the West Street side of the cemetery. At this 1868 meeting, the conversation started on the possibility of building a vault, which was later built in 1870 by Dedaker & Miller for $1,200.

In 1871, a committee was formed to attain counsel due to the coming day when Montgomery Avenue was to be widened. At a meeting in 1872, the trustees, just off their success with building Palmer Vault, began talking of building a new bier house, a building that would contain a bier (a movable stand on which a corpse, often in a coffin, is placed prior to burial).

With income coming in from rental properties, internments and vault fees, the board of trustees' treasury reached over $1,000, an amount they had not seen since the 1810s. At this time, longtime trustee Daniel Dwier Sr. died. He was replaced by John Dwier on July 30, 1872. Dwier was no doubt a relative, if not another son, of Daniel's. Daniel Dwier Jr. was still serving on the board.

In 1873, city planners finally got around to widening Montgomery Avenue. Since widening the street took away a portion of the cemetery's land, the city compensated the cemetery with $3,500. This money was used by the trustees to pay for the construction of the "Bier's House." Today, the bier house is the only structure still standing within the cemetery.

The trustees meeting that was held on July 30, 1873, was the meeting during which the trustees reported how they spent the $3,500.00 compensation from the city. They paid off Verdier & Richards for building the bier house; they paid to have bodies removed from along Montgomery Avenue for that portion that the city was claiming ($24.00); and they also paid to advertise the removal of bodies ($8.40). Their attorney James Page was paid $399.23 for his services in dealing with the widening of Montgomery Avenue; the trustees also paid Samuel Hall & Son $562.12 to move back the house that sat at 1400 Montgomery Avenue. Later in the year, the trustees spent close to $1,500.00 on new curb stones and paving.

Also at this July 1873 meeting, they hired a new gravedigger, A. Getz, to replace longtime gravedigger John Myers, who had died. Since the management of the cemetery now included several rental properties, a vault, a bier house, plus the regular internments, the trustees decided that they should meet quarterly.

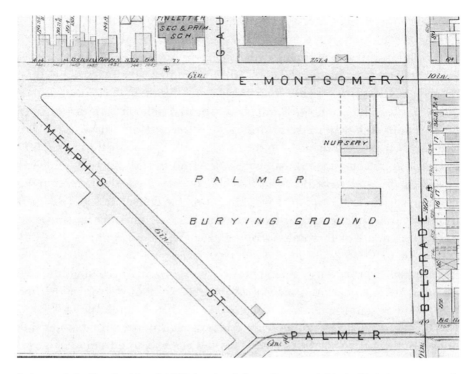

Snippet of the *Bromley Atlas of 1887* showing Palmer Cemetery's Vault, Krebs's nursery and the 543 Belgrade and 1400 Montgomery Avenue rental houses still standing.

In October 1874, the trustees had three hundred feet of iron fencing put up along the line of what would become Memphis Street. The cemetery now had iron fencing on most of three sides, except Montgomery Avenue, which had none. July 1876 finds Frederick Krebs making his first appearance in the record of Palmer Cemetery. Krebs, a florist, rented the house at 543 Belgrade and would eventually build a large nursery on the cemetery's grounds.

In April 1877, it was announced that longtime trustee Daniel Dwier had died. He had been a trustee since 1839, almost forty years. Also in April, the trustees found out their compensation for the opening of Memphis Street and the taking of a piece of their property. The damages compensation was $2,290.

By this point in the cemetery's history, the trustees had purchased three lots over the years, so they could expand the cemetery, but then they lost land twice with the widening of Montgomery Avenue and by the cutting through of Memphis Street. It only remained for the trustees to buy a small triangular piece of ground at the northwest corner of the burial ground for the cemetery to finally reach the dimensions by which we know it today. This purchase, from the estate of George DeHaven, took place in 1884. The trustees paid $1,000 for a triangular lot less than seventy-one feet on the long end.

Finding a replacement for Daniel Dwier proved difficult. The trustees had two elections with no results, the first in their history. Each trustee wanted to vote for their own candidate. On the third try, they were finally able to elect John Hague. Hague was from an old Kensington family who owned a good deal of land eastward of the cemetery. The Hagues were also related to the Day family (Andrew Day had previously sat on the board). Joseph Paxson at this point was elected secretary and treasurer. Albert Emerick remained on as superintendent of the vault. George Baker was the president.

In 1878, the trustees finally got around to contracting the completion of the iron fencing on a stretch of Memphis Street that wasn't finished yet, as well as the entire length of Montgomery Avenue. Other added features that the trustees splurged on, since their treasury was top-heavy in the late 1870s and 1880s, was to have Moritz supply marble posts and railing on the south side of the center carriage way from the vault to the corner and from tree to tree. They also planted flowers on the lawns of the rental houses, removed the old house (Lower House) at the corner of Belgrade and Palmer, filled in the area and graded it. They made this southeast corner of the cemetery available for burials in 1882 and in 1883 built a fountain in the middle of the schoolhouse

Photograph (pre-1964) of Palmer Cemetery, taken from a house on Montgomery Avenue, showing the nineteenth-century wrought-iron fence that used to surround the cemetery. *Courtesy Daniel Dailey.*

A view of the oldest part of Palmer Cemetery taken from Fishermen's Hill and looking out toward the asphalt brick path that leads to gates along Montgomery Avenue.

lot. The trustees also continued on with their practice of not charging for burials for women from the Penn Widow's Asylum (today's Penn Home).

Alexander Fountain died in 1880, to be replaced by Jacob Jones. In January 1881, John Hague became president, Joseph Paxson remained as secretary and treasurer, Albert Emerick remained as superintendent of the vault and A. Getz remained as gravedigger. In March 1881, it was announced that Conrad Baker had died. He was replaced by Edward Willig. In October 1881, 355 yards of asphalt paving blocks were laid down in the paths of the cemetery at a cost of $710.

The trustees kept getting offers in from various individuals and organizations. At one time (1880), they declined a $500 offer for perpetual care for Jane Hardy's family grave and then accepted it later. Another time they denied the W.S. Newhall Post No. 7, Grand Army of the Republic (GAR), in building a "Soldiers Monument" on the cemetery grounds but later allowed the building of a World War I monument.

A committee that was set up to draft bylaws and rules delivered its report on July 28, 1884. The cemetery would now be governed by further written rules, plus the deed of trust. At this point, the cemetery was still called the Kensington Burial Ground. The new rules called for the "new burial" areas to be kept in actual order, unlike the old part of the cemetery—each grave was to be three feet wide, with tombstones the same. The new burials would start consecutively from the north path on Palmer Street.

There were new prices for burials, and vault fees were also spelled out in the bylaws and rules report of 1884. Adults without a case were to pay $4.00, $4.50 with a case and $6.00 with a casket. For children from seven to fifteen years in age, the cost was $3.00, $3.50 and $4.25, respectfully. For smaller children, under the age of seven, it was $2.50 without case or $3.00 with a case or casket. Vault fees were $3.00 for the first week and $0.75 per week after the first week, with one month maximum storage time. These new rules also created the title of superintendent of the cemetery (different from the vault superintendent), which simply gave the gravedigger a new title, with the same responsibilities. Burial requests were to be given to the superintendent at least twenty-four hours in advance.

A rather odd occurrence took place on April 16, 1885. Pennsylvania declared the day Arbor Day and requested that people plant trees. The trustees purchased from nurseryman Thomas Meehan of Germantown (who was instrumental in helping to create Penn Treaty Park) eight Norway spruces and planted them on the schoolhouse lot in the cemetery. The square lot had one tree planted in each corner and then four at the points of what would be a diamond shape that was within the square that the other trees fashioned but also surrounding the fountain in the center of the lot.

Normally, this would not be so odd, but for some reverential reason, the trustees named the trees after themselves, plus one each for Getz the superintendent and Reverend Hervey Beale, a local popular Presbyterian minister. Also in 1885, more artificial (asphalt) blocks were laid down, and the superintendent of the cemetery was to now perform the duties of handling the vault as well. David Emerick, a relative of trustee Albert Emerick, tried to run for the newly expanded position of superintendent, but received only one vote to Getz's four votes. Finally, in 1887, the rest of the carriage paths were completed with the asphalt blocks.

Soon after Getz beat Emerick in the election for superintendent, he resigned due to another business opportunity he had. After another election, Albert Emerick Jr., the son of the trustee, was voted the new superintendent. Jacob Jones had nominated "Mr. Stoop," who was probably one of the Stoop brothers who were superintendents of Hanover Burial Ground.

In 1887, the trustees meeting minutes book became filled. A new book was ordered to be purchased. The year 1890 brought the death of Joseph Paxson, the secretary and treasurer of the board of trustees, and John Dwier, who for many years had been a member of the board. G.W. Price was voted to replace Paxson. David Emerick was voted to take the place of Dwier. With the addition of David Emerick, it made three members of the Emerick family serving for the cemetery at the same time: President Albert Emerick, Superintendent Albert Emerick Jr. and David, the newly elected trustee.

The year 1890 also saw the trustees put flagstones down as a path in the new part of the cemetery (southeast corner). Albert Emerick was elected president, and John Hague became secretary and treasurer. In 1892, the secretary and treasurer positions were split, with Hague remaining as secretary and Edward Willig taking over as treasurer. Albert Emerick Jr. remained superintendent. Ornamental gates were installed at this time on Montgomery Avenue; the Palmer Street gates had already been installed.

The Montgomery Street iron gates; although local folklore states that these gates were imported from England, there is no evidence in the cemetery's archive to prove this.

While these gates are stated today to be from England, there is nothing mentioned in the trustees meeting minutes that noted this.

The sidewalks along Belgrade Street were paved with flagstone in 1894 at the cost of $648.47. In 1895, newly elected trustee of 1890, G.W. Price, died and was replaced by John Price. Later in the year, David Emerick died. James Dougherty was voted to replace him. About this time, all of the trees on Belgrade Street and Palmer Street that had been planted by earlier trustees were taken down by the then current board, for which no reason was given.

The end of the nineteenth century came to the cemetery with the destruction of a section of the bier house due to a fire. In April 1899, it was stated that the tool house and porch of the bier house were destroyed by fire; however, they were insured, so there was no expense to the cemetery. There was no mention of any records of the cemetery being destroyed nor any mention of new books or ledgers needing to be purchased. The cemetery's records had previously been kept in the "fire-proof safe" that was housed at one of the trustees' homes, usually the secretary or treasurer.

BURIAL RECORDS FOR PALMER CEMETERY

From 1765 to 1817, individual internments do not appear to have been kept, only the number of burials and money paid. For the period of 1818 to 1832, no records at all appear to have been kept, either. A legend has been handed down that states that when the bier house caught fire in 1899, records were lost. However, a close reading of the trustees meeting minutes shows that there was no book kept, at least during the period when the new board was formed in 1839 and the order to purchase a book for interment recordings was made in January 1860. From 1817 to 1833, there are no records at all, but this appears to have been due to the disintegration of the board, not from some sort of destruction, especially when you see that the cemetery ledger stops at 1817 and picks up again in the same ledger in 1833.

There were burial permits that were printed up and filled out by individual trustees, and for the most part these are lost and are probably the only "internment" records ever kept at this time. These slips were filled out by the trustees, signed by a witness and handed over to the gravedigger, later the superintendent. The Palmer Cemetery archive only has three burial permits from 1864 and eighty-nine permits for burial from 1865. However, these deaths are covered more fully in the internment records that exist for these years. There are only three burial permits that have survived prior to 1860, one for 1834 that is unreadable, one for Aderline Rice from 1840 and one for Elizabeth McKinney in 1850. Internment registers starting on August 1, 1859, and continuing to the present exist.

RENTAL PROPERTIES ON THE CEMETERY GROUNDS

When the trustees of Palmer Cemetery purchased the second lot from Christian Sheetz, it came with three rental houses already built on it. These eighteenth-century structures had seen better days and were in need of repairs and renovations. By June 1802, the three houses start to show up in the original register of the cemetery's trustees as being rented out.

The three houses on the cemetery grounds were identified in the registers as the Lower House, Middle House and Upper House. When the city required putting addresses on buildings, these homes became 509 Belgrade Street, 543 Belgrade Street and 1400 Montgomery Avenue.

The Lower House was rented from the time the trustees had acquired it until they were forced to file a legal notification on May 21, 1880, for the tenants' removal due to issues of back rent. About 1884, the trustees had the Lower House taken down and removed. The area around the house, from Palmer Street north to the vault, from the eastern edge of the schoolhouse lot to Belgrade Street, was "filled up and graded and laid out with walks &c for burial purposes."

The Middle House stood at 543 Belgrade Street at the southwest corner of today's Belgrade and Montgomery, with the Upper House sitting behind it on Montgomery Avenue. The house was generally rented to a series of German families, particularly ones in which the head of the house was a gardener and could perform work from time to time for the cemetery.

At the board of trustees meeting of July 31, 1876, it was announced that Frederick Krebs would be renting the grounds and building out of which Albert Gast was moving. The rent would be $240 annually, payable monthly at $20.

Krebs had arrived in America just before he started to rent at the cemetery. He was a florist and established his floral business when he took up on the grounds of the Palmer Cemetery. Previously there had been two occupants of the Lower House, George Bechtell and John B. Feldon, who were gardeners, as was Albert Gast, who had lived at the Middle House before Krebs. Krebs appears to have joined this list of German gardeners.

Cemetery rental houses: 543 Belgrade Street, with 1402 Montgomery Avenue in the background. Image shows Ida Haigh and child, June 27, 1939. *Courtesy Urban Archives—Temple University.*

Krebs took a lease for five years, and in April 1880 he asked the board of trustees to extend his lease another six years, which the members did. However, when it came time to renew the lease again in August 1886, the board of trustees were not willing to renew Krebs's lease for another five years, but rather they allowed Krebs the option to remain for a year with the additional option to renew yearly. This might have been due to the cemetery filling up—the trustees did not want that section of the cemetery tied up in a contract for another five years in the event that they needed it.

A letterhead of Krebs's from the 1880s reads: "Fred. S. Krebs, Florist, Bedding Plants and Cut Flowers, 543 Belgrade St., and Montgomery Av." The *Bromley Atlas of 1887* shows Krebs's nursery as being built in the northeast corner of the cemetery, behind and next to the home that he was renting at Belgrade and Montgomery. The nursery was quite substantial, perhaps a square quarter of a block, running along Belgrade Street from about Eyre Street to Montgomery and from Belgrade westward almost to Miller Street. The Palmer Vault sat at the southwest corner of Krebs's nursery. Krebs did tree trimming work for the cemetery, as well as selling flowers on a number of occasions to decorate the lawn of the schoolhouse lot.

Frederick Krebs continued to rent the burial ground property up until he died on October 24, 1906. After the death of her husband, Mary Krebs stayed on renting at the cemetery. Trustee minutes show her paying rent up until at least 1911. At about this time, the trustees wanted to use the land

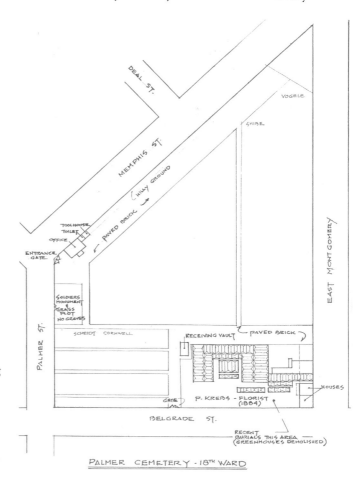

A 1940s map drawn by Charles R. Barker showing the historic features of Palmer Cemetery, including the bier house (office), the vault, Krebs's nursery and two rental houses.

where the nursery stood for burials and dismantled it. By the time the *Bromley Atlas* was published in 1910, the nursery had been dismantled or demolished and the area opened up for burials; however, the 543 Belgrade Street home remained into the later half of the twentieth century, with many old-timers of the neighborhood remembering it. When repair work was being done on it in the late 1950s, or early 1960s, it was noticed that the building had been put together with pegs, showing its ancient age. The house was still standing in 1976 but is now gone.

The Upper House, 1400 Montgomery Avenue, was also rented out to a series of German families, often widows. In 1946, the trustees took out insurance on the 1400 and 1402 East Montgomery Avenue properties

A view of the northeast corner of cemetery, showing the crowded conditions of the "youngest" section of the cemetery, which was once occupied by Krebs's nursery.

for ten years. In 1969, water bills were still coming in for 1400–1402 East Montgomery Avenue. This 1402 East Montgomery Avenue house must have been part of the 1400 East Montgomery Avenue house and then turned into a separate unit at some point. It does not show up in the records until very late in the nineteenth century. Dennis Shane published his pamphlet on the cemetery's history in 1976 and mentioned that this 1400 Montgomery Street house was still standing.

OTHER STRUCTURES ON THE PALMER GROUNDS

Nuskey's Rope Walk

Besides the three houses that were on the Christian Sheetz lot along Belgrade Street, the cemetery once owned the Everhard Bolton lot that sits today underneath Memphis Street. The lot measured 40 feet on Palmer Street and 168 feet, 3 inches along the western edge of the cemetery. This lot was purchased by the trustees with the thought of expanding the cemetery. However, they never used the lot for burials but rather rented it out; later in the nineteenth century, it was condemned by the city when Memphis Street was brought through.

Casper Herbell started to rent the "lot on Palmer Street" in January 1839 during the time that he was the gravedigger at the cemetery. He used it as a garden. The lot rented for fifteen dollars annually. In March 1841, Herbell started to rent a second lot on Palmer Street. He was given both lots for twenty dollars per year. Perhaps the trustees had divided the property.

Casper Herbell died during the summer of 1847. His wife, Ann Herbell, took over the lots on Palmer Street. She immediately started to do work at the cemetery to help defray the cost of the rent, so she could keep the garden going. She was paid $19.52 on July 28, 1847, for "whitewashing the fences including Lime and Brushes." In March 1849, Ruben Giberson, son-in-law to Ann Herbell, paid her rent for the period of March 1849 to February 1850. This is the last entry in the cemetery's treasurer's account book for Herbell.

Jacob Dumer for a time rented this Palmer Street lot, and after he gave it up, the trustees rented it in 1860 to John Nuskey, a rope maker. Nuskey built and operated a ropewalk on the lot. He originally rented the property for five years, starting on February 1, 1860. After the five-year agreement ran out, the trustees of Palmer Cemetery renewed a lease for the property for three years with Lewis Nuskey, a relative of John's. The trustees, knowing that there might be a possibility of Memphis Street coming through the property, or even of Palmer Street being widened, wrote into the three-year lease that they would not be held liable for any damages if these types of incidents occurred. The lease was for only the land on which the frame ropewalk building sat, not the rest of the land surrounding the building on the lot.

The ropewalk was carried on until Lemon (Memphis) Street was brought through in late 1876. The street was thought to have come through the lot for many years before it finally did.

The Palmer Vault

The first trustees meeting during which the Palmer Vault was mentioned was July 28, 1868, when Daniel Dwier motioned that a committee be appointed to research the cost of erecting a vault. On February 18, 1870, the committee reported back that it had estimates from Dedaker & Miller and George Kelly. Liking Dedaker & Miller's proposal, the trustees entered into a contract with this firm for the construction of the vault for $1,200. By January 31, 1871, Dedaker & Miller had been paid in full.

Albert Emerick was appointed the first vault superintendent and given a salary for his troubles. Emerick was a good choice for the superintendent's position; he lived right at the southwest corner of Palmer and Belgrade. This January 31, 1871 meeting also saw the first income received for vault fees, $57.00, thus the vault must have been operational sometime in late 1870. The vault became a very good moneymaker for the cemetery. By July 1871, the trustees reported an income of $116.45 for vault fees. Of this amount, Emerick was paid $32.25. Like the gravedigger, he received a fee for every occasion that the vault was used.

The only records that have survived for the vault are two thin volumes. One volume is dated August 6, 1871–January 25, 1874. The other volume, only eight pages long, is dated January 27, 1886–June 4, 1887. These vault records usually list the name of the deceased, age, date when placed in the vault, the undertaker and how much was charged.

According to the bylaws of the burial ground, the remains of persons who died of smallpox or other contagious diseases were not deposited in the receiving vault. The bylaws stated that the charge for bodies deposited in the vault was $3.00 for one week, plus $0.75 per week after the first week until removed. No bodies were allowed to remain in the vault for a time longer than one month from the date of depositing. Satisfactory security was given for the removal of the bodies. The superintendent had full charge of the vault to receive all bodies and see them delivered to the proper parties without charges.

The vault was erected halfway between Montgomery and Palmer. From a map created by Charles R. Barker, the Palmer Cemetery Vault is shown being located roughly on what would have been the north side of Eyre Street if Eyre Street ran through the cemetery instead of stopping at Belgrade Street. The cross position was located between the third and fourth tiers of graves from the Belgrade Street side. The vault was set partially underground. It sat at the southwest corner of Krebs's nursery and had steps leading down into it.

In 1878, the trustees installed a marble roof on the vault, but in order to install this they needed to have a cornice laid first on the brickwork to rest the roof on. They also contracted with Mr. Moritz to put an ornamental frontispiece on the top of the vault. The large "PALMER" stone that sits presently at the corner of Belgrade and Palmer Streets within the cemetery was this "ornamental frontispiece." It originally sat on top of the vault. There was an iron railing added around the vault later on.

The vault also appears to have been rather roomy, as it is reported at one trustees meeting in January 1883 that there were ten bodies presently in the vault. It was also a popular place—records showed seventy-two bodies laid in the vault between January 29 and April 30, 1883. In 1885, the superintendent of the cemetery took charge of the vault as well.

The vault lasted for just over a century. In 1975, with a build-up of kerosene fumes along with old rags being stored in the vault, plus the participation of some juvenile delinquents, the vault exploded. The roof caved in and the PALMER stone crashed to the ground. The explosion destroyed the vault. The remains were shoveled into the underground portion of the vault, and it was buried over. When the roof of the vault collapsed, the PALMER stone was moved to different places in the cemetery and then finally to its present location.

While the vault might have physically lasted until 1975, it was not in use for all of those years. It appears to have stopped being used years before it was taken down, possibly as early as the 1930s or 1940s, if not earlier.

The Bier House

While not mentioned in the earliest trustees meeting ledger of Palmer Cemetery, a later ledger stated that there was once an old bier house at Palmer and Belgrade Streets prior to 1843 and that this house was moved to the western side of the cemetery, back from Palmer Street. It would later be taken down to be replaced by the current structure that sits at the corner of Memphis and Palmer Streets.

After the success of the building of the Palmer Vault, the trustees then set about the building of a new bier house. The first meeting during which it is mentioned was on January 30, 1872. A bier house generally has a bier stand on which you would place a coffin prior to burial.

On November 18, 1872, a special meeting was convened to hear the bier house proposals. Three bids were received: Richards & Verdier, $1,350; Samuel Hall, $1,390; and Hall & Filmann, $1,675. The board decided to go with the cheapest bidder, Richards & Verdier.

Verdier appears to have been a local house carpenter who lived at 600 Susquehanna Avenue, near today's Memphis Street. He is probably the same Verdier who worked as Verdier & Kepler and who had been hired by the cemetery previously to do carpenter work back in 1862.

Richards, the other member who helped build the bier house, is not as easily identifiable. He could possibly be Thomas Webb Richards, an architect who

The Palmer Cemetery bier house, built November 1872–73 by Richards & Verdier at the cost of $1,350. A cinder block addition was added on later.

had worked for a time with Samuel Sloan, a noted Philadelphia architect. Perhaps Richards was known to trustees of the cemetery through his work with Sloan, as Sloan had locally designed the First Presbyterian Church of Kensington on Girard Avenue, Episcopal Hospital on Lehigh Avenue and the old Gorgas School that had once sat on Susquehanna at Belgrade. If this was Thomas Webb Richards, soon after this project he moved on and became the first professor of architecture for the University of Pennsylvania, later designing College Hall among other buildings at the university.

The building's architectural style is such that it appears that an architect, and not a regular neighborhood carpenter, designed it. It is reminiscent of a popular late nineteenth-century style carried out by the likes of Frank Furness. Unfortunately, not enough evidence has been found at this point to render a positive verdict for it to have been designed by Richards.

This new bier house was also used by the superintendent of the cemetery as storage for his tools, and it also acted as an office for the cemetery, a place where the trustees could hold their meetings.

Chapter 6

Palmer Cemetery in the Twentieth Century

WORLD WAR I MONUMENT, EIGHTEENTH WARD WELFARE ASSOCIATION AND ELM TREE POST NO. 88

The twentieth century brought two world wars to America. While the cemetery was not greatly affected by World War II, World War I changed the look of the cemetery, as for the first time the trustees allowed something to be built on the schoolhouse lot (excluding the previous small fountain that was placed there).

On July 1, 1919, a meeting was held at the Soldiers & Sailors Recreation Room at 410 East Girard Avenue. The purpose of the meeting was to "organize a Post of the American Legion for the service men of the 18th Ward who had been in the service of the United States of America during the great struggle, inclusive of the following dates: April 6, 1917 and November 11, 1911, and who would be known as the World War Veterans of the 18th Ward."

After the formation of the post, an election was held to name the post. "Elm Tree Post" won out. Twenty months after formation, it is reported by the Elm Tree Post on February 10, 1921, that the Eighteenth Ward Sailors & Soldiers Welfare Association had opened up communications with them and wanted to meet. Trustees David Muir and Oliver Kerr and post historian Howard Stinson formed a committee and met with the Eighteenth Ward Welfare Association.

Purchased by Elm Tree Post No. 88 in 1921, 1414 Palmer Street sits across from the cemetery and is the former home of lumberman Alexander Adaire.

On February 14, 1921, the committee reported back to the Elm Tree Post, stating that the Eighteenth Ward Welfare Association wanted to erect a monument in Palmer Cemetery in memory of war heroes and wanted Elm Tree Post to work with the organization. Kerr, Stinson and William Leper formed a committee that would work on this project. They had no power to act but were simply instructed to wait on the welfare association and report back its actions.

At this time, Elm Tree Post members had been meeting at a building owned by Post No. 7. captain W.S. Newhall, GAR, at Eyre Street and Girard Avenue, and was looking to purchase a building of their own. They purchased 1414 Palmer Street, the former home of Alexander Adaire, a local state legislator, president of the Philadelphia Lumber Exchange and member of the Philadelphia School Board. The first meeting in their new building was held on April 14, 1921. This building was located directly across the street from Palmer Cemetery where the World War I memorial was to be built.

ᴄArmistice Day Celebration
KENSINGTON
Friday, November 11, 1921, at 1 p. m.

UNVEILING MONUMENT IN PALMER CEMETERY

Soldiers' and Sailors' Welfare and Citizens' Committee
will unveil Bronze Tablet in memory of the men who served
their Country in the World War

MONSTER PARADE AND DEMONSTRATION WILL PRECEDE THE MEETING

ROUTE OF PARADE – Start East Girard Avenue and Aramingo Avenue, along Girard
Avenue to East Montgomery Avenue, to Memphis, to Palmer, to
Girard Avenue, to Second. Countermarch on Girard Avenue, to Columbia Avenue, to
Frankford Avenue, to Palmer, to place of unveiling.

ALL CITIZENS ARE REQUESTED TO DISPLAY THEIR FLAGS

An invitation card to the unveiling of the World War I monument dated for Armistice Day,
November 11, 1921. *Courtesy the trustees of Palmer Cemetery.*

The World War I memorial arch built on the schoolhouse lot. The cornerstone was laid on
October 29, 1921, by the Eighteenth Ward Sailors & Soldiers Welfare Association.

On October 29, 1921, the cornerstone of the granite memorial arch for fallen World War I veterans was laid at Palmer Cemetery by the Eighteenth Ward Welfare Association. William Rowan—president of the board of education and a popular local undertaker who performed many burials at Palmer Cemetery—was chairman of the exercises. Rowan was also instrumental in the founding of Penn Treaty Park in 1893. More than five hundred people attended. A plaque with the names of thirty-nine men from the neighborhood who lost their lives in the war was affixed to the monument.

The arch was built on the lawn of the schoolhouse lot. In the nineteenth century, a previous Palmer Cemetery Board of Trustees rejected the idea of a war memorial when proposed by the GAR.

CAPTAIN HARRY PRICE, COMMANDER OF THE HARBOR POLICE

Starting in the 1920s, Penn Treaty Pier (Pier 57), located within Penn Treaty Park, became the home of a unit of the Philadelphia Harbor Police, as well as a fireboat unit. The merchant marines also had a training ship, the *Annapolis*, that docked at Pier 57. On June 7, 1931, the park made the news when this unit of the harbor police had a boat explode at the foot of Columbia Avenue. The superintendent of police, William B. Mills, as well as six harbor policemen were hurt. The boat, named for the superintendent, was on a trial trip and exploded as it pulled into Penn Treaty Park. After little more than two decades, the harbor police and fireboat units were relocated.

One of those injured policemen eventually died from his wounds. Captain Harry Price, commander of the harbor police, had his leg crushed and was severely burned. He was admitted to St. Mary's Hospital but died thirteen days after the explosion on June 20, 1931, at the age of forty-nine. He was buried in Palmer Cemetery.

REBIRTH OF THE BOARD OF TRUSTEES

An article published in the *American Cemetery Magazine* in July 1964, entitled "Neighborhood Committee Restores Ancient Philadelphia Cemetery," stated that "until about thirty-odd years ago, the Kensington Burial Ground was well maintained." This would seem to indicate that up until the 1930s the cemetery was well taken care of and then fell on hard times. As we have seen previously with the board of trustees, the enthusiasm only lasts a couple of decades at a time; the spirit of the World War I memorial board apparently did not carry over to the 1930s and 1940s.

During the Depression, the city assigned some WPA work crews to the cemetery, but their efforts failed. It was said that some of the large older trees fell and smashed the iron fencing that circled the cemetery. These gaps in the fence were patched with wooden pickets. Juvenile delinquents set fire to the

Graves of the family of marble man Jacob G. Fennemore who took the trustees to court in 1902 in order to build his own headstone foundations for his family's graves and won.

undergrowth, smashed and overturned tombstones and busted out the windows of the caretaker's house. The cemetery was filled with poison ivy, rodents and insect colonies. Garbage and debris littered the place. The final blow came with Hurricane Hazel in 1954. Twenty-seven of the larger trees were blown down. The damage from the falling trees was great, vaults were smashed and memorial stones were destroyed.

According to the *American Cemetery* magazine article, everyone in the neighborhood was disgusted with the cemetery, but nobody did anything. Then one day, while two men were having a conversation across the street from the cemetery, the talk turned to the condition of the cemetery. They decided to do something about the deplorable state. They started in the area in front of their houses (Montgomery Street), and with sickles and grass whips they trimmed out the undergrowth. One of these men was Albert Dailey, grandfather to current trustee Daniel Dailey.

Albert E. Dailey, one of the men who started renovations of the cemetery in the late 1950s and early 1960s, shown painting an eagle for the Bicentennial. Courtesy Daniel Dailey.

After a short time, others began to join them until they were a force of men and women amounting to about two dozen people. They would work their day jobs and volunteer at the cemetery after work or on the weekends. Slowly they began to restore the cemetery. About fifteen of the volunteers developed poison ivy. They had no money to expend on the project, so they used their own tools.

After doing what they could with their own hands, the time finally came when they needed to raise money to buy windows in order to restore the caretaker's house and buy new lawn mowers and grass whips. A fundraising committee was founded. Ray Liebowitz, the commander of the Elm Tree American Legion post, became the chairman of the committee, James Downs became the secretary and George Shrives became the treasurer (the article refers to him as "the late George Shrives," thus he must have died prior to July 1964). Helen Ruoff became treasurer upon Mr. Shrives's death.

The fundraising effort was successful through contacting local businesses and descendants of those buried in the cemetery. The temporary committee was replaced by a permanent organization that directed the improvements and maintenance of the cemetery. William Sweeny was elected president; Jim McCue, vice-president; and Harry Masterson, co-treasurer and custodian. Martin Ruoff, Jim Early and Charles Hock were named as trustees.

The new organization took down what was left of the iron fence, first installed in 1885, and replaced it with a new chain link fence, keeping the original gates. The total cost to fence the cemetery amounted to $4,000. While not as attractive as the iron fencing, figuring out how to pay for a new fence was paramount to aesthetics at that time, and it was much cheaper to sell the iron fence for scrap ($517) and add that money to their efforts to pay for the new $4,000 fence.

A cinder block toolshed was built as an addition to the old bier house. Walkways were restored, and seventy-five trees were planted, most coming from donations by supporters of the restoration of the cemetery. An old rental building at Montgomery and Belgrade was also restored, receiving new glass in the windows, painting inside and out, a new roof and weatherboarding. While the men were working on the structure, they discovered that it had been put together with pegs. This building was rented out again, and the income was used for the upkeep of the cemetery.

The next project was completed in the fall, and it included a new pavement on the Montgomery Street side for at least half of the block at a cost of $2,600. All four sidewalks, running completely around the cemetery, ran about $13,000.

The cemetery received money on several occasions from local churches, which donated their entire Thanksgiving collections to them, amounting to $247.90. Women from the Republican Club donated $10.00. A "County Fair" was held at Penn Treaty Park, and the ice cream sales and "wishing well" raised another $75.00 for the cemetery. The women of the restoration committee conducted an annual house-to-house canvass of the neighborhood and were successful in raising further money for the cemetery.

The article from 1964 stated that 25 veterans of the American Revolution were buried in Palmer, 1,300 Civil War veterans, five Spanish-American War vets and three veterans of World War I. At that time (1964), it was said that there was room enough for 1,000 more burials. According to this article, Harry Masterson was a key part of the renovation of the cemetery.

William Price, a reporter for the *Philadelphia Inquirer*, toured the cemetery just after all of the renovation work had been completed:

> *Today the clean marble tombstones stand erect at Palmer Cemetery. The lawn is verdant and lilies and geraniums grow alongside the fence. Oak, willow and mimosa trees provide color and shade, while fragrant pine shrubs are spread throughout the cemetery, which has regained the label, "pride of the neighborhood," and stands as a tribute to the hardworking residents.*

As much work as went into restoring Palmer Cemetery in the late 1950s and early 1960s, only a short ten years later the cemetery was again beginning to decline. Several letters to the editor that were published in the *Penn Treaty Gazette* (forerunner to the *Fishtown Star*) on August 13, 1975, complained of the poor condition of the cemetery. Margaret and Linda Clinton both wrote letters to the *Gazette* complaining of the disgraceful condition of the cemetery. The complaints stated that the grass was so overgrown that you couldn't see the tombstones. It was also at this time that vandals destroyed the Palmer Vault. There is also a photo in this issue of the *Gazette* showing Mrs. E. Pieifer and her grandsons Harry and Scott cleaning up the debris that had gathered along the Memphis Street side of the cemetery.

The letter campaign to the *Penn Treaty Gazette* seems to have paid off. The noise that was created about the cemetery created a stir. By November 1976, the *Penn Treaty Gazette* was reporting on the restoration efforts that were underway yet again on Palmer Cemetery. Not only was the board of trustees again motivated to make improvements to the cemetery, but individuals and business helped out as well. In November, the Penn Treaty Bicentennial

The Palmer Cemetery Board of Trustees in 1977, with Shackamaxon Street resident and U.S. Congressman Raymond F. Lederer (third from left). Longtime president James D.B. Weiss is at far right.

Volunteers cleaning up the cemetery during "Pitch In," an anti-litter campaign. *From left to right*: Mr. Sebzda, Joe Brozo, Chris Dailey, Steve Custer, March 27, 1976. *Courtesy Urban Archives—Temple University.*

Committee presented the Palmer trustees with a check for $1,500 that was to be used for the restoration of the bier house and the care of the grounds then and into the next spring.

The new board of trustees in 1977 was made up of Steve Pascavitch, president; Lewis Stevens, vice-president; Helen Barth, treasurer; Dennis Shane, secretary; and James D.B. Weiss Jr., superintendent. Of this group, James Weiss is the only one still involved with the Palmer Cemetery as of 2010.

The president of the trustees, Steve Pascavitch, was quoted as saying, "We really need a constant flow of funds since we don't want the work to slack off. We'd like the community to take an active part in beautifying the cemetery." While the restoration work was gradual, signs of the work were beginning to be noticed. The trustees placed temporary markers for the recent burials at times when the family was unable to place a grave marker. However, local vandals were still plaguing the cemetery, tearing up these markers for

The grave of "Fishtown's Brightest," Debbie Szumowski (1954–2003), editor of the *Fishtown Star*. She was a tireless promoter and advocate for the neighborhood, beloved by all.

no good reason. Secretary Dennis Shane pleaded with the public to stop trashing the cemetery.

The trustees planned regular fundraisers and asked for donations as well from the community. One task they were trying to accomplish was to replace the brick sidewalk along Memphis Street with concrete. The brick sidewalk needed too much repair. The trustees themselves renovated the bier house as a way to save the money that would have went to a contractor. A new award was established by the trustees, the Anthony Palmer Award, to be given to "those persons who dedicate their service to the Fishtown-Kensington communities and in particular, the Palmer Cemetery."

At the end of the twentieth century, burials at Palmer Cemetery began to slow down. For the period of 1976 to 2007, there were about 837 burials that took place. The average was about 27 burials per year for this thirty-one-year period, or about two per month. The high point in burials during this period was 1994 with 44, and the low year was the last year, 2007, with only 8 burials. The years between 2004 and 2007 showed a steady decline in burials.

Palmer Cemetery in 2010

As the twenty-first century dawns on Palmer Cemetery—as well as the prospect of the burial ground being a couple of decades away from being three hundred years old—the reality is setting in that it will soon not be able to accommodate any more burials in the very near future, if not already. Cremations will probably have to be the alternative.

An example of the overcrowded conditions of the cemetery is the odd way of determining where someone can be buried, which was described to this author by James D.B. Weiss, the longtime president of the board of trustees. The family chooses a spot, and a long aluminum pointed pole is used to poke the ground in various spaces to see if there are any obstructions; if there are no obstructions, they can be buried. If there are obstructions, you need to move to another location and keep poking. The cemetery is that crowded.

Weiss's family has lived in Fishtown for more than one hundred years. He stated that the current boundaries for those eligible to be buried in the cemetery is a little larger than the original boundaries and that they now accept those living in the triangle formed by the Delaware River, Frankford Avenue and York Street. These borders differ from those of the 1976 board of trustees, whose boundaries were the "Delaware River to Frankford Avenue to Wildey Street to Front Street to Palmer Street to Frankford Avenue to York Street to the Delaware River." Both of these sets of boundaries were expanded to the boundaries of what most natives of the area would call the boundaries of the Fishtown neighborhood.

Both sets of these boundaries are much larger than the original boundaries of the 1765 deed of trust, which would have been the original Palmer grounds (the Fairman estate) on which Palmer built his town of Kensington. Those early borders were Hanover (Columbia Avenue) Street at the Delaware River west to Frankford (Avenue) Road, north to Norris Street, east to West (Belgrade) Street, north to York Street, east to Gunnar's Run (Aramingo Avenue to Dyott Street), down the course of the creek to the Delaware River and then south on the river to the place of beginning at Hanover Street. It might also have taken in the three lots that sat in a triangular shape west of Frankford Road between Hanover and Norris Streets. These larger boundaries set by the later boards of trustees, which have been the norm since before 1976, allowed many more burials than were expected by the original trustees, perhaps leading to the present crowded conditions of the cemetery. This, plus the attempts by later trustees to lay tiers like in a traditional cemetery, with footpaths and such (which take up more room), all make for further crowded conditions.

It is sad to think that after all these years Palmer Cemetery might close its doors to burials. The cemetery will still be there, but what usually happens to a cemetery once it stops accepting burials? History shows that the income of the cemetery is reduced, family members of the deceased in the cemetery die off, the cemetery starts to fall into disrepair, people start to complain, someone gets the notion to condemn it and then another person starts calling for the removal of the bodies to reuse the land for a more modern purpose.

While a small foundation exists for the cemetery, how long can it possibly last without an additional source of revenue? Hopefully the trustees' decisions will become more transparent to the community, and this will allow for larger participation and a bigger potential for raising the necessary funds to secure the cemetery's future. As the history of Palmer Cemetery has shown, the cemetery has had boards of trustees that were very good (1850s–1870s, 1960s–1970s) and some that were not so good (1810s–1830s, 1930s–1940s). How will history judge the current board? Will Palmer Cemetery remain the treasure that it has been for generations? Or will future Kensingtonians and Fishtowners experience it only by reading this book?

Chapter 7
Hanover Street Burial Ground

KENSINGTON ME "OLD BRICK" CHURCH AND THE FOUNDING OF THE HANOVER BURIAL GROUND

On September 27, 1825, at a board of trustees meeting of the Kensington ME Church, trustee George C. Schively proposed that the church should buy a lot for a burial place, situated on Hanover (Columbia) Street between Duke (Thompson) and West (Belgrade) Streets.

At the Kensington ME trustees meeting of January 18, 1826, a motion was made for "James Mickle & Mathias Creamer" to be "appointed a committee to obtain the necessary signatures to enable the trustees to carry into effect the proposition of George C. Schively, relative to the lot for a burying place." The next day, Mickle and Creamer reported to the trustees that they had received thirty-four signatures of members assenting to the purchase of the burial place. These signatures represented two-thirds of the male members of the church. A motion was then passed to purchase the lot for a burial ground, and a committee was formed for that purpose, with the authority to carry it out.

The treasurer's report lists $353.56 given to the committee for the burial ground. In Reverend Swindell's history of the church, he reported that the church paid $700.00 for the burial ground on Hanover Street. At a trustees meeting on June 17, 1826, a motion was made to build a tool house on the new burial ground lot. By March 27, 1826, income had started to be recorded ($128.50) for funerals at the "new ground," even though it does not appear to have been officially open yet. Money was also still coming in from Kensington ME's "old ground." The church also paid $24.00 in interest on the loans for the new burial ground.

A committee was formed on May 22, 1827, to draw up a plan for the new burial ground on Hanover Street, made up of George C. Schively, John Bennett and James Mickle. The committee worked on its plan over the course of the summer and fall of 1827. In early 1828, they had the deed to the new cemetery recorded, and the cemetery planning committee had reported back; progress was made, and a new committee was established to oversee the workings of the cemetery and to sell the lots. The lots were to be sold for fifteen dollars each. George C. Schively, William Bennett and David Clayton comprised the first supervisory committee for Kensington ME Church's new cemetery at Hanover Street.

On March 27, 1828, it is recorded that $165 was taken in by the church in funeral monies. There is no longer a designation of "old ground" or "new ground," so it is hard to tell if the members were still burying people at the "old ground" at Marlborough and Richmond Streets.

By July 15, 1828, it was reported that the tool house had been completed, a small bier house had been finished and fencing had been started. Later, on July 22, a motion was introduced to build a house on the burial ground lot, to be used for occasional committee meetings and for accommodating families at funerals in bad weather. Signatures were gathered for approval from two-thirds of the male members, and on July 29, the resolution was adopted to erect a building eighteen feet by twenty-four feet on the burial ground.

In 1829, a gravel walk was constructed on the new burial ground, and the schoolhouse was rented out to "Brother Ware," provided that he would let it be available to people at funerals in inclement weather.

The minutes of the trustees in November 1829 seem to indicate that Jacob Ware was renting a "house" on the Hanover Burial Ground and using it as a "school room," perhaps running a private school. The trustees raised his rent to thirty dollars per year, and Ware decided to give up the schoolhouse. This schoolhouse was rented later to Samuel Adams in March 1835 and then to Admiral Ward in June 1835.

By early March 1832, the monies for the old and new burial grounds were reported together, thus it is not possible to see how many burials actually took place at the older burial ground. It would probably be correct to state

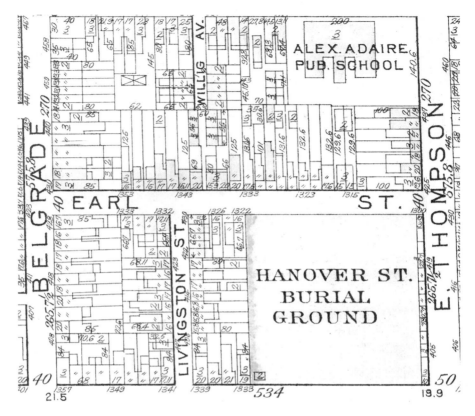

Snippet of the *Bromley Atlas of 1922* showing Hanover Street Burial Ground and the cemetery superintendent's house, plus the ramshackle wooden houses along Thompson Street.

that there were no more burials at the churchyard at this point and that all the burials were now being moved to the Hanover Street lot. The churchyard was next to the church at Marlborough and Richmond Streets. The following April the trustees decided that the poor members of the church who could not afford to bury their dead would be paid for by the church and that the expense would be paid back to the church.

By early April 1833, Kensington ME's business agent for Hanover, Matthias Creamer, was reporting a balance in the burial ground's account as being $351, a large amount back then. The cemetery certainly appeared to be helping the church with income, as this money was paid over to the church secretary who, in turn, placed it in the church treasurer's hands.

Kensington ME Church only took up one-third of Hanover Burial Ground. Its lot had frontage on Hanover Street of one hundred feet going

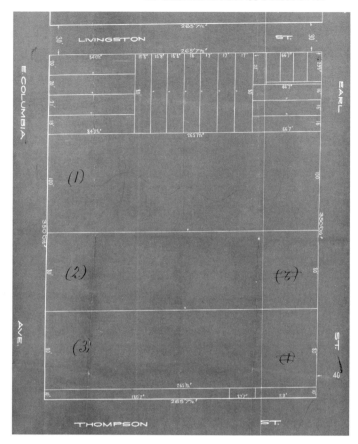

The plan of Hanover Street Burial Ground showing cemeteries within it: (1) Kensington ME Church; (2) Union Wesleyan Church; and (3) Union Harmony. *Courtesy Kensington ME Church Archives.*

back to Earl Street at right angles. The other two-thirds of Hanover Burial Ground was taken up by Union Wesleyan Methodist Church and Union Burial Ground Company, which each had an eighty-foot frontage on Hanover Street, also going back to Earl Street at right angles. We will now take a short look at these two cemeteries.

Union Wesleyan Church

According to Rich Remer, who wrote a brief history of the Union Wesleyan Church, the origins of the church go back to the appointment of Reverend Samuel S. Kennard as pastor of Kensington ME "Old Brick" Church in the year 1824. Remer went on to state:

84

In his [Kennard] *own words, "shortly after conference, it was evident that Days of Grace were not far distant some were awakened and a few converted, while a general quickening appeared among the members. About the 1st of August, 1824, our expectations were even more than realized. A glorious and powerful revival commenced, which has continued to the present time, April 12, 1825."*

Remer also stated that

[the] *spiritual event, however, caused strains within the church membership for by July of that year, in the words of a later pastor* [Reverend W. Swindells], *Brother S.S. Kennard, for certain personal reasons, left the church and organized an independent Methodist church, and built a frame church on Richmond below Shackamaxon Street. A few sympathizers followed him, but the Society had a brief existence.*

Reverend Swindells is not exactly telling the whole truth. While it is true that the church did not last that long on Richmond Street (only ten years), it did, in fact, last a very long time; it is still in operation as the Pilgrim Congregational Church, located today at Belgrade and Marlborough Streets.

Swindells also mentions that "a few sympathizers" left with Kennard. However, records show that sixty-four members of Old Brick Church went with Kennard, a nice-sized proportion at that time for the church. These sixty-four members and Reverend Kennard formed in August 1825 as the Union Wesleyan Church. Within two weeks of the succession, Remer stated that eighteen additional members of Old Brick left to join Union Wesleyan. More than 20 percent of Old Brick's membership left to join Reverend Kennard, much more than the "few sympathizers" mentioned by Reverend Swindells.

The new church was erected on property belonging to Joseph Ball, an original member of the church and, by marriage, an uncle of Reverend Kennard. Ball descended from William Ball, who owned much of today's Port Richmond neighborhood, known in olden times as the Hope Farm estate. The property where the church was built was actually the property of Ball's infant daughter, Harriet Ball, so the church never did actually own the land. Remer stated that the verbal agreement that Joseph Ball had with the church to be located on his daughter's property fell apart after his sudden death. Harriet Ball's guardians thought otherwise of using the young girl's property for the church, and ten years later in 1837, the church had to move from Richmond Street.

Through Rich Remer's research, we find that Reverend Kennard was married back in January 1827 to Mary Pruitt Hodgson, the daughter of Robert and Ann Hewson Hodgson. Ann was the daughter of John Hewson, the Kensington Revolutionary War hero and calico printer who is buried at Palmer Cemetery. The day after Reverend Kennard was married, Richard Farmar Bower was ordained a minister of the Wesleyan United Society and joined Reverend Kennard. Bower was a member of family who owned the old Bower Mansion house on Frankford Avenue, just below Norris Street. Kennard did not survive to see the fruits of his labor. He died thirteen months after marrying. Reverend Bower took his place as head of the church.

The Union Wesleyan Church joined the Conference of Associated Methodist Churches, later called the Methodist Protestant Church. When the church had to be moved from the Richmond Street property in 1837, the congregation purchased a lot at Belgrade and Marlborough Streets, on the northwest corner. They dismantled the church, and with the school they rebuilt and settled at the new lot, organizing anew as the First Associated Methodist Church of Kensington in December 1838.

At the time, the church recorded the deed for this new church property, Reverend Bower was gone and Reverend John G. Wilson had taken over. In 1851, another spilt took place within Union Wesleyan, now known as First Associated Methodist Church of Kensington. Reverend Wilson started another new church of fifty-nine members called Salem Methodist Protestant Church of Kensington. This new church was located on Dunton Street, near Girard Avenue.

First Associated still had 120 members left according to Remer. These members reorganized themselves, with Reverend Wilson's help, as the Ebenezer Meetinghouse or Church or as the Ebenezer Independent Christian Church. On January 24, 1885, Reverend John G. Wilson died. He had been the minister of the church for more than forty-five years.

Temporary pastors filled the void left by Reverend Wilson until 1896, when H.W. Myers Jr. was elected permanent pastor. He stayed as pastor of the church for many years and helped guide the church through a good part of the first half of the twentieth century. It was under Reverend Myers that the church was reorganized yet again and came to be known as Pilgrim Congregational Church, evolving into the name used today, the Pilgrim Congregational United Church of Christ.

Hanover Street Burial Ground

Back in 1830, Union Wesleyan, when it was still located on Richmond Street, acquired a section of Hanover Burial Ground for its cemetery. The lot that the members acquired was the "northern moiety" of a lot that was spilt in two evenly with the Union Harmony Burial Ground. This section of Hanover was the middle section, with the westernmost section being owned by Kensington ME Church and the easternmost section belonging to Union Harmony.

The northern moiety of the lot was conveyed by deed of indenture bearing the date August 5, 1830, by Jacob Fisher, Jacob Hineback, Daniel Bispham, Robert Hodgson, Jacob Andress and Robert Lynn, to "the Wesleyan Church of Kensington" as and for a graveyard. The whole of this lot (both northern and southern moieties) was held by Fisher and the others in trust for Union Harmony "until their incorporation or appointment of trustees for the same" and for the "Wesleyan Church" aforesaid as by a certain declaration of trust bearing the date of July 14, 1828. Fisher and the others had acquired this lot in 1828 from Samuel Brick.

A tax ledger exists in the archive of Kensington ME Church for the lot holders of that portion of Hanover Cemetery that had belonged to Union Wesleyan Church. This ledger includes an alphabetical index at the front and then individual pages for the lot holders. While the lot numbers run between 1 and 206, there are actually only 132 lot holders, with one of these being the trustees of the cemetery. Of the 206 lots, there are only 162 that have names associated with them; 3 lots were owned by the trustees. There were 44 lots uncounted for. Thus, it's not clear just how many lots were in the Union Wesleyan Church's section at Hanover Cemetery. Did they all eventually fill up? Unfortunately, we have not yet found burial records for the section of Union Wesleyan Church at Hanover. Due to the age of the cemetery, the many splits and reorganizations of the church and more, the records probably no longer exist, but we hold out hope.

Each page for the tax register of lot holders includes the name of the lot holder and the tax per year for the lot for the years between 1861 and 1899. The tax was a consistent twenty-five cents per year. The tax does not appear to have ever been collected regularly. There are long lapses of not paying and then a person might pay for the past twenty-five years at once.

The handwriting style, the type of ink used and the entries in the register all appear to give the impression that this *Lot Holder Tax Record Register* was established in 1884, with earlier entries being backdated at that time (1884) to bring the accounts up to date. Nearly everyone (all but twelve) paid the tax in 1884, with only occasionally taxes for previous years being paid and most people paying the taxes after 1884.

It would seem that someone sought out the lot holders in 1884 asking for the taxes due, perhaps to help with the upkeep of the cemetery. This might account for the forty-four unknown lot holders; perhaps these owners were never found.

The year 1861 is given as the starting date for every lot holder, so perhaps the lot tax was started that year, but no one ever paid. Entries kept after 1890 are in a different hand, and the ink is different. In the back of the book, after the entries for lot holders, is one manuscript leaf that shows tax collections between August 9, 1879, and October 21, 1887. The total collected for this time period was ninety dollars on thirty-eight different accounts. Of these thirty-eight accounts, two of them are recorded as having paid on two different occasions. All of these payments were for past due accounts, the debts ranging from two to twenty-three years old. None of these accounts on this page is for the "missing" lot holders.

The inside front of this ledger contains the name "E.C. Brown, 1933 N. Fifth St., Phila., PA." Presumably this is the person who started and kept this tax ledger between 1884 and 1890, giving it up to someone else afterward—or perhaps the person who might have taken over in 1890 was E.C. Brown. It's unclear.

There is mention in this tax register ledger of Union Wesleyan, at the front, in a small penciled note that states: "Shibe doing up grave July 26th, Baseball people." This note presumably relates to cleaning up, or fixing up, the grave of John Shibe, or his lot, at Union Wesleyan Church's cemetery. There is a John Shibe who owned Lot No. 182 at Wesleyan. Benjamin F. Shibe, onetime half-owner of the Philadelphia Athletics baseball team and the founder of Shibe Park, was a native Fishtowner. His father was John Shibe, and he also had a brother named John Shibe. It's unclear which John Shibe this is, but the mention of "baseball people" with the name of "John Shibe" certainly associates this John Shibe with Ben Shibe's family.

Union Harmony Burial Ground

On June 1, 1831, Christopher Dilman, George D. Henk and Mathew Robinson were the signatories to transfer ownership of the plot of ground that would become Union Harmony Burial Ground into the hands of the president of Union Harmony Burial Company of Kensington, James

McCormick. Dilman, Henk and Robinson were all described as "yeoman" of Philadelphia County. Union Harmony was represented by its president, McCormick. Dilman, Henk, Robinson and McCormick all had burial lots at Union and used them for either themselves or their families.

The cemetery plot was transferred over to McCormick for one dollar. Dilman and the rest were holding the property in a deed of trust; their attorney was Jacob Coleman. The lot was described as

> *beginning at a stone in the side of Hanover Street corner of James Hartley's lot marked in a certain map or plan number five, thence by said Hartley's lot north sixty seven and a half degrees east two hundred and sixty five feet and five inches to another corner of said Hartley's lot numbered thirty three in the said map and bounded on a street forty feet wide, thence by the said street south twenty one degrees east one hundred and sixty feet to a corner of John Brick's senior lot marked in said plan number forty two, thence by said John Brick lot south sixty seven and a half degrees west two hundred and*

A row of wooden trinities that once lined the eastern edge of Hanover Street Burial Ground along Thompson Street. These houses were only ten feet in depth.

sixty five feet and five inches to a corner of said John Brick's lot number fourteen on said map, thence along said Hanover Street north twenty one degrees west one hundred and sixty feet to the place of beginning, containing about one acre be the same more or less, including in the bounds lots six, seven, eight, nine, then, eleven, twelve, thirteen also thirty four, thirty five, thirty six, thirty seven, thirty eight, thirty nine, forty, forty one, as numbered and marked in the said general plan.

It would appear that the map, or plan that is mentioned, was for the dividing up of a family estate. The lot was divided up into at least forty-one different lots, encompassing the block bounded by Earl, Thompson and Hanover Streets, with Hartley and Brick having the lots on each side of the cemetery lot. The lot that Union Harmony was acquiring was the "southern moiety" of the lot described, or the southern half of the previously described lot with an eighty-foot frontage on Hanover Street, going back to Earl Street at right angles. The other half, the "northern moiety" as described above, was acquired by Union Wesleyan Methodist Church. Fisher and the others deeded in trust to Dilman and the rest to hold for Union Harmony. By the time the plot was finally turned over to Union Harmony, Henk had died. Dilman and the rest empowered Jacob Colman to make the deeds to convey property to Union Harmony. Union Harmony became incorporated on March 3, 1831, thus they finally acquired the land on June 1, 1831. The deed was recorded on July 23, 1832.

THE HELVERSON FAMILY AND THEIR OWNERSHIP OF UNION HARMONY BURIAL GROUND

Nicholas Helfenstein (circa 1789–1859), later Helverson, was born in Pennsylvania. He was the founder of the family undertaking business. Early on he was listed in the Philadelphia city directories as a carpenter, and as late as the directory of 1835–36 he is listed as a cabinetmaker. However, starting in 1836 he was advertising in Philadelphia newspapers as a "Furnishing Undertaker and Coffin Maker" at the "S.E. Corner of Coates [Fairmount] & St. John [American] Streets." This advertisement in the *Public Ledger* also stated that Helverson was the "superintendent of several Burial Grounds, where internments can be had." An obituary for Mary Sylvania in the *Philadelphia Inquirer* of July 19, 1848, was already calling Union Harmony the "Helverson's Burying Ground, [at] Hanover Street, East Kensington."

By 1859, Helverson's two sons, William (1820–1900) and Horatio (circa 1829–1871), were advertising that they would continue the business of the "late N. Helverson, Undertaker, at the old stand, 225 Coates St." However, the partnership did not last—two years later, on July 17, 1861, the Helverson brothers were advertising that the partnership had been dissolved by mutual consent and that "Horatio S. Helverson will conduct business at the old stand, 225 Coates St., above St. John. Wm. S. Helverson will conduct business at the N.E. corner of Coates and St. John St."

Horatio began calling himself the "successor to the late Nicholas Helverson" since he conducted his business from the building where his father previously was located, even though his older brother William was located across the street from him and also conducting an undertaking business. By 1871, Horatio had died, and William appears to have become the main Helverson conducting the funeral business, even though there were others (nephews and so on). By 1900, William had brought his son, also William, into the business, changing the name to William S. Helverson & Son. He had moved to 939 North Tenth Street, where he was located when he died on August 10, 1900. William Jr. took over the family business. It was his son who removed the bodies from Union Wesleyan and Union Harmony when Hanover Burial Ground was closed.

Besides their funeral business, coffin-making business and various positions as superintendents to local burial grounds, the Helverson family also had some sort of financial interest in the Union Harmony Ground, a burial ground within the Hanover Cemetery. Nicholas Helverson was also involved in another local Kensington cemetery, the Franklin Cemetery Company, where he is found as one of the signatories to an act to incorporate this burial ground on May 29, 1840. He also had involvement in the Mutual Burial Ground of Kensington mentioned later in this book.

KENSINGTON ME's MANAGEMENT OF THE BURIAL GROUND

Kensington ME Church registers for its burial ground at Hanover records both Union Wesleyan and Union Harmony as paying water rent to Kensington ME. This would seem to indicate that either Kensington ME was the only one of the three to have access to water and thus availed it to the other two for a fee or Kensington ME was actually the one that managed Hanover Burial Ground.

The vault at Hanover Cemetery was owned by Kensington ME Church, since it sat on its portion of the cemetery, and it is shown in the records of the church as charging fees for its use. The Kensington ME cemetery account ledgers show the church paying for repairs to the vault. It also repaired the pavement along Earl Street in 1902, the sidewalk along Columbia Avenue in 1906 and the cemetery gates in 1916 and papered the cemetery house in 1916. From all of this it would seem that Kensington ME Church managed the Hanover Burial Ground.

Further evidence is shown by the various superintendents of the cemetery, who were paid by Kensington ME Church. One such superintendent was Andrew Stoop (circa 1837–1916), who worked at the cemetery from at least November 1900 to October 1915. He was a Civil War veteran. Stoop had been a gravedigger since at least 1860.

Charles Stoop, Andrew's brother, is shown by the Kensington ME records as working at the cemetery from about 1882 to 1900, having started out

Photograph of Hanover Street Burial Ground taken from Columbia Avenue, undated. The large building in the background is the old Adaire Elementary School. *Courtesy Daniel Dailey.*

Photograph of the superintendent's house at Hanover Street Burial Ground, undated. The vault stood north of the house. *Courtesy Daniel Dailey.*

digging graves and eventually taking over as superintendent, living at the cemetery house. While Charles Stoop worked longer at the superintendent position at Hanover, Andrew Stoop appears to have been the last superintendent of the cemetery before it was closed. Ann Stoop, the mother of Charles and Andrew, lived at the cemetery house as well, and when she died she was buried at Hanover.

THE BEGINNING OF THE END OF KENSINGTON ME CHURCH'S CEMETERY AT HANOVER

The Kensington ME Church had been overdrawing on its accounts for a number of years before the sale of Hanover Burial Ground. The members frequently needed to tap into the endowment fund to pay their expenses and then hopefully pay back what they borrowed in order to not shrink the endowment.

The heyday of the church appears to have peaked, and now the slow decline had begun. The summer of 1917 saw the church starting to downsize. At the trustees meetings they started to mention the selling of the big parsonage home at 1117 Shackamaxon in order to find a more suitable (smaller) place for the pastor. It was finally sold in 1922, the same year that Hanover Cemetery was closed.

Up until just about the closure of the cemetery, the cemetery was still bringing income into the treasury of the church, but it was also costing the trustees money to maintain. As late as March 1919, the house at the Hanover Burial Ground was being rented out to a woman for six dollars per month, with the income paid into the "Saving Fund" of the church. There was no longer a superintendent, the city having condemned the cemetery, slating it for removal. This same month it was reported that the pavements around the cemetery were in disrepair and needed to be fixed. By September, the burial ground agent had reported that the repairs were taken care of.

At a meeting on November 24, 1919, the possibility was first mentioned that the church would move from its longtime location at Marlborough and Richmond Streets because of the future needs of the church and the fact of the widening of Delaware Avenue. It was advised that a special fund be created in the event that the church did choose to move, and a special meeting was called for the congregation to discuss the issue.

At this time in the history of the church, trustee Harry W. Loeble acted as the burial ground agent. At a trustees meeting of September 4, 1920, it was resolved that the burial ground agent would have full power to act on any business concerning the cemetery. An annual report of the church for the year ending February 1920 showed that the church took in from the Hanover Burial Ground a total of $72.00 from March 1919 to February 1920. The expenses for the cemetery included water rent (1918–19) at $10.75, the pavement repair work at $10.75, a new hydrant put in at $10.00 and snow removal costs of $4.50. The balance on hand for the cemetery was $36.00.

A meeting of the congregation was held on February 8, 1921, to discuss the possible relocation of the church. Pastor Rowland Garber spoke at length, picturing the church after the widening of Delaware Avenue was completed. He thought that it would be "unsafe for any lady to travel on or near [Delaware Avenue] after nightfall." After much discussion, it was decided to create a building fund, to be established and ready if the opportunity presented itself to move the church.

With the treasurer's report for February 1921, there is a record of the burial ground agent handing in $100, showing that the cemetery, while supposedly condemned by the city, was still generating income.

The Decision to Close the Cemetery

There is no mention in the trustees meeting minutes about the church being approached by the City of Philadelphia in order to condemn Hanover Burial Ground and turn it into a recreation center. However, on June 10, 1921, at a meeting of the trustees of the church, it was mentioned that a committee was to be formed in order to secure the services of a "good lawyer to look after the interest of the church in connection with our portion of the Hanover Burial Ground." Several months later, on November 8, 1921, it is recorded at a trustees meeting that the pastor, Rowland Garber, was appointed as a committee of one, in regards to the removing of the bodies and other business concerning the burial ground. It was apparently thought best to have one individual (Reverend Garber) deal with this delicate matter of removing the remains of the loved ones of local residents—who better to deal with it than the pastor of the church?

It appears that this issue was not discussed all that much by the board, perhaps because it was the city that wanted the cemetery condemned, so it

Photograph of Hanover Street Burial Ground in its last years before removals took place, circa 1922. *Courtesy Urban Archives—Temple University.*

was not really a decision that the board of trustees had to debate. This same November 8 meeting showed a deposit of $23.54 into the church's treasury from the burial ground, thus income from the burial ground was still coming in as the trustees discussed the various aspects of closing it.

On December 13, 1921, the treasurer was given permission to place a deposit on the property that was to be selected (when the time came) by Pastor Garber (as a committee of one) for the reburial of the Hanover Cemetery remains. On March 22, 1922, a bid from undertaker Frank Dreher was accepted to remove the bodies from Hanover, and on March 26, a committee was formed to scout for a cemetery to remove the bodies to and to purchase the necessary amount of lots.

Sign posted at Hanover: "The City of Philadelphia has taken over this property... All bodies must be promptly removed." It's unclear what the burlap bag is for.

As required by law, the Kensington ME Church put notices in the local newspapers of the *Public Ledger* and the *Legal Intelligencer* on April 21, 1922. Those notices read as follows:

COURT OF QUARTER SESSIONS FOR THE COUNTY OF PHILADELPHIA.
In the matter of the Removal of the Dead from the Burial Ground of the Kensington Methodist Episcopal Church on Columbia Avenue, Thompson, Earl and Livingston Streets, in the 18th Ward of the City of Philadelphia.

Notice is hereby given to all parties interested, that the Court of Quarter Sessions entered a decree on April 7, 1922, directing the trustees of the Kensington Methodist Episcopal Church to procure lots in the Forrest Hills Cemetery, Byberry, Philadelphia County, Pennsylvania, and to remove the dead buried in the burial ground of the Kensington Methodist Episcopal Church, at Columbia Avenue, Thompson, Earl and Livingston Streets, Philadelphia, and bury the same in the lots so purchased at the Forrest Hills Cemetery, at the expense of the Kensington Methodist Episcopal Church, and that the burial ground of the Kensington Methodist Episcopal Church on Columbia Avenue, Philadelphia, be forever vacated for burial purposes: Provided, however, that relatives and friends of such dead shall have the right to remove said remains, at any time, at their own expense, before actual removal by the said trustees; and, pursuant to said decree, notice is hereby given to all such relatives and friends that the trustees are proceeding forthwith to remove said remains, and that if such relatives and friends desire to exercise the right to remove the remains of any of their dead, said relatives and friends should communicate immediately with Dr. Roland J. Garber, 1117 Shackamaxon Street, Philadelphia, Penna. FRANCIS SHUNK BROWN, Attorney for the Trustees of the K. ME Church.

REMOVAL BID FOR HANOVER'S KENSINGTON ME CHURCH'S BURIAL GROUND

While not mentioned in the trustees minutes, there was committee work going on that was not reported, usually noted simply as "Burial Ground Committee reports progress." Letters exist in the archive of Kensington ME Church that showed this "progress." The "progress" was that Memorial Parks and Mausoleum Company of Pennsylvania, the parent company that operated Forest Hills Cemetery and Mausoleum Park, solicited a bid to receive the remains of the Kensington ME Church's Burial Ground at Hanover Cemetery. In a letter dated March 17, 1922, Adolph Hoch, a manager with Memorial Parks, wrote to Reverend Rowland G. Garber, Kensington's pastor, and proposed a bid of one hundred or more lots at the price of twenty-seven dollars per lot including, one opening. All of the other openings were to be charged at the rate of seven dollars per opening. The entire plot was to be kept under "Perpetual Care." The size of the lots was to be seven feet by ten feet, with a pathway of three feet between each tier of lots.

Kensington ME liked the proposal but had questions about how many extra boxes could go in a grave and how large the actual graves were. In a return address of March 31, Hoch responded to Kensington ME's questions by stating that there would be a "free opening in each lot to be for a full size grave, accommodating any size case that may be shipped." It was also understood that in each grave would be placed two internments. Thus, while indeed the removals would be a mass burial, there would be no more than two cases placed in each seven- by ten-foot lot.

Pastor Garber was given permission by the trustees to purchase lots in Forest Hills Cemetery. By May 11, 1922, Kensington ME responded to Memorial Parks (Forest Hills) with a deposit of $300 to start the project. A sketch of the design of the plot that accompanies this correspondence collection shows Forest Hills' idea for the section of lots for the Kensington ME Church's removals from Hanover. It was to be a simple grid pattern of two tiers of graves, each tier being twenty lots long by two lots wide, making forty burial lots for each tier. The tiers were divided by a three-foot pathway. The number of internments sent by Kensington would determine how many tiers would be used; the design shows two tiers. Regardless, each two- by twenty-lot tier would have three-foot pathways on all sides.

STARTING THE REMOVAL

A month later, in May 1922, officers of the treasury of Kensington ME Church were given instructions to borrow up to $10,000 for use of the burial ground and the task of closing the cemetery, removing and reburying the bodies. It was also noted that Pastor Garber was given the authority to allow one grave instead of a "lot" for people holding deeds who had not come forward up to that point or shown any interest in the Hanover Burial Ground.

In the treasurer's report of June 13, 1922, it is reported that the trustees paid $800 to Forest Hills for one hundred cemetery lots that were needed for the Hanover removals. They also paid the undertaker, Frank Dreher, a total of $3,000 in two payments totaling $1,300 and one of $1,700 for the removal of bodies and noted that this job was completed. To cover these costs, the church borrowed $2,000 from the Kensington National Bank and $1,000 from the William Cramp & Sons Savings Fund, as well as used $800 from its "Building Fund," the fund that was established to use in the event that members decided to move the church.

The law firm of Brown & Williams was used to handle the negotiations with the City of Philadelphia for the Hanover Cemetery property. The church received $62,596.70 for the property. While not handling the case pro bono, Brown & Williams charged only a small fee to help the church. This money received by the church from the city was put into the church's building fund account.

The final tally for the expense for Kensington ME Church for closing Hanover Cemetery was $2,282.00 for Forrest Hill Cemetery for the one hundred lots and reburial; $7,000.00 to undertaker Frank Dreher, who removed the bodies at Hanover, boxed them and carted them to Forrest Hills; and a $500.00 bonus to the church's pastor Garber for overseeing the operation. During the removal process, Garber kept a detailed notebook of all of those bodies that were removed and where they were placed at Forrest Hills. These records are presently held by Kensington ME Church. There was also a minimal cost for some tombstone work that was needed. The total cost of the project was $9,824.50, or just under the $10,000.00 the trustees had budgeted.

During the removal process, the contractors fenced the cemetery with boards "to keep the exhuming of the bodies from the view of the public." All of the bodies were "placed in boxes constructed to the rules of the Board of Health, hermetically sealed, pitched and rubber between the box and box lid."

In a letter on June 17, 1922—addressed to Mr. S.E. Kuen, assistant title officer of the Real Estate Title Insurance & Trust Co., and written by Francis Shunk Brown, the lawyer for Kensington ME Church—Brown assured Kuen that all of the removals had taken place, had been witnessed by Kensington ME's Reverend Garber and had been inspected during the process by the City of Philadelphia's Board of Health director C. Lincoln Furbush. Everything was carried out in good order and approved, and all those who helped plot deeds were fully satisfied. Brown then asked Kuen to issue the mandamus policy by the next day, so that the property could legally be transferred over to the city.

Brown also informed Kuen that the city had condemned Hanover Cemetery for burial purposes "about 15 years ago, and since then there have been no burials made therein." This estimation of Brown's would seem to be off by six to eight years, as records seem to show burials still taking place as late as 1915–16.

A final note that dealt with the cemetery removal was that Pastor Garber handed over to the trustees for safekeeping fourteen deeds for Forrest Hills Cemetery lots that were not used, meaning that of the one hundred lots they purchased only eighty-six were actually used. Tally sheets that still exist in the archive of Kensington ME Church seem to indicate that there were at least three thousand bodies in the cemetery, but it doesn't appear that this many bodies were removed. If each lot was to hold two graves, one hundred lots would only total two hundred graves. However, if a grave was to be one coffin filled with bones, then it is possible that a wooden coffin could be filled with several bodies' worth of bones.

Barker, in his work on Philadelphia cemeteries, stated that Section No. 30 of Fernwood Cemetery was where Union Harmony and Union Wesleyan removals were taken. He also went on to state that there were some remains removed to Graceland Cemetery in Yeadon, Pennsylvania, and that the then secretary of the board of Yeadon, Mrs. L.W. Elliot, had the records (1940s). Also, it has been reported that some bodies were removed to North Cedar Hill Cemetery in Philadelphia. At the time of George R. Barker's research on this cemetery, he talked with a local contractor, George Vaughn, of East Montgomery Street, who told him that some gravestones from Hanover Street Burial Ground were used in constructing some of the homes on Susquehanna Avenue, presumably as foundation stones.

A WINDFALL FOR THE CHURCH'S TREASURY

No sooner had the money that Old Brick received for Hanover Burial Ground been placed in the church's "building fund" account than it was being used to pay salary and bonuses for the pastor, whom the trustees thanked for overseeing the closing and removal of the bodies at the cemetery.

The treasurer was ordered by the trustees to make sure that all bills were paid. The trustees then took off for the rest of the summer, perhaps finally relaxing knowing that the treasury of the church was in better shape than it had been for a long time.

The church trustees used some of the money from the sale of the Hanover Cemetery property to acquire properties at 1200–1208 Marlborough Street and 252 East Girard Avenue. They bought these properties in the event that they were needed to move the church. While the church trustees waited to see if they would move or not, they rented out the properties, which brought in close to $900 per month, a nice investment. The church never moved and is still located at the same spot at Marlborough and Richmond Streets, where it was founded 206 years ago as of 2010. They sold the Marlborough Street properties a while back.

Along with the money paid to Kensington ME, the trustees of the Union Wesleyan Burial Ground and the trustees of the Union Harmony Burial Ground of Kensington each received $60,464.10. The owners of the row of wooden ramshackle houses along Thompson Street received less than $11,000.00, with the brick homes along Livingston Street and the couple of homes on Columbia Avenue and Earl Street receiving on average about $2,500.00 each.

REMINDERS OF HANOVER BURIAL GROUND

While the Hanover Burial Ground was closed and the bodies removed in 1922, reminders of the cemetery still pop up from time to time. On October 2, 2002, Joe Volpe and Frank Conroy of General Asphalt Paving Company were working at Hetzell's Playground installing a sprinkler system for the ball playing field. While the two men were digging, they found a tombstone for "Susan Hugg," a six-year-old girl who had died December 21, 1850. The tombstone was very readable and in very good condition. It had been buried about two feet underground on the Earl Street side of the playground. A search of the internment records for Kensington ME Church's portion of the Hanover Burial Ground does not find Susan Hugg being buried there during that time period, thus she must have been buried in one of the other two sections of the cemetery belonging to either Union Wesleyan Church or Union Harmony Burial Company.

Tombstone unearthed at Hetzell's Playground

Joe Volpe (top photo left) and Frank Conroy were surprised to dig up an 1850 tombstone belonging to a six-year-old child, Susan Hugg. /Small

An October 2002 newspaper article about an old tombstone that had been unearthed during the installation of a sprinkler system at Hetzell's Playground, the old Hanover Street Burial Ground.

The men put the tombstone back where they found it, thinking that they may have disturbed the young girl's grave. The story got out in the neighborhood that the tombstone had been found, and a reporter for the *Fishtown Star* newspaper showed up at the playground. The men unearthed the tombstone again to show the reporter. Upon consulting with one another, they decided to remove the tombstone and deposit it at Palmer Cemetery.

Chapter 8

Union Burial Ground of the Northern Liberties and Kensington

A Place of Many Names

This burial ground is also known as West Street Burial Ground, Union Burial Ground of Kensington, Malt House Ground, German Burial Ground and Thumlert's.

THE MULTI-NAMED CEMETERY

The Union Burial Ground of the Northern Liberties and Kensington once sat on the south side of Vienna (Berks) Street between West (Belgrade) and Gaul Streets. It operated roughly from 1831 to 1892, although burials were supposed to have been stopped in the 1870s. The cemetery over the course of its more than fifty-year history was known by at least six different names. Getting to know the various names of this cemetery will help you to be able to identify whether your ancestors were buried at this location and what possibly might have become of their remains.

The cemetery took on the name of "West Street Burial Ground" due to the fact that its eastern border was West Street, an earlier name for Belgrade Street, and the most popular street of any of its locations. West Street became Belgrade Street in 1858. For the purposes of the history of this cemetery, we will call the Union Burial Ground of the Northern Liberties and Kensington by its shorter nickname, West Street.

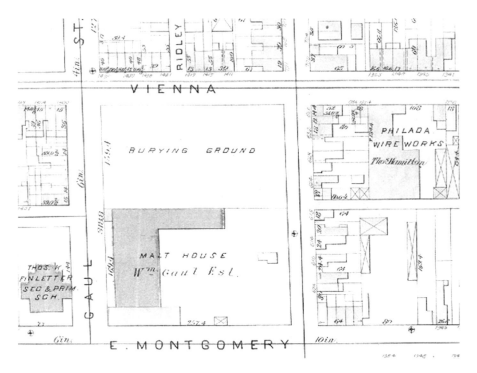

Snippet of the *Bromley Atlas of 1887* showing "Burying Ground" at the location of the West Street Burial Ground, north of William Gaul's (Gaul Street) Malt House.

All of the founders of the West Street Burial Ground came from the District of the Northern Liberties, which sat just south of Kensington. Horatio B. Pennock, a merchant, is said to have granted and conveyed an acre of ground for the burial ground to Jacob Stearly, Anthony Shermer and Joseph R. Paul on May 6, 1831. Stearly, Shermer and Paul all appear to have already been involved with the Union Burial Ground Association, as they were listed as the trustees for that group. Presumably the West Street Burial Ground would be another cemetery for this society for the Kensington and Northern Liberties section of the then Philadelphia County.

The original trustees of the West Street Burial Ground (Jacob Stearly, Joseph R. Paul and Anthony Shermer), to whom Horatio B. Pennock transferred the acre of land in Kensington, were all from the Fifth and Sixth Wards of the District of Northern Liberties.

According to Barker, the Philadelphia Board of Health has cemetery returns for the period of 1838 to 1860, and during this period it is called

Union Burial Ground of the Northern Liberties and Kensington

"Kensington Union." For some reason, the cemetery even shows up being called the "German Burial Ground" on the *Hopkins Atlas of 1875*. There were a number of cemeteries in 1875 in this part of Kensington, and Hopkins simply may have made a mistake in the naming of it.

Because of the cemetery's association with the Union Burial Ground Association, it also came to be known as the "Union Burial Ground," and since it sat north of and next to Frederick Gaul's Malt House, it was also at times known as the "Malt House Ground."

Another name the cemetery went by in later years was Thumlert's, after one of the caretakers of the cemetery. George Thumlert (1818–1908) was also an undertaker and is said to have buried the poor for free. Thumlert also may have owned a bit of the cemetery later on in its history, and thus the cemetery was sometimes referred to by his surname.

Thumlert was also from the same Sixth Ward of the District of Northern Liberties where several of the original trustees of the West Street Burial Ground were from, and thus he presumably would have known the trustees since he was in the undertaking business and since the trustees were involved in the Union Burial Ground Association. Thumlert was born in 1818 and died on October 1, 1908.

One of the three original trustees of West Street Burial Ground, Jacob Stearly, was from Northern Liberties' Sixth Ward. In the 1850 Census, he was listed as a brewer with a personal estate worth about $10,000. It's possible, due to his background in the brewing business, that he knew Frederick Gaul and knew of the availability of the land next to Gaul's Malt House, which is where the West Street Burial Ground came to be located.

The second trustee, Joseph R. Paul, was also found in the neighborhood of Northern Liberties' Sixth Ward and worked in some capacity as a clerk.

The third trustee of the burial ground, Anthony Shermer, resided in Northern Liberties' Fifth Ward. He was a cabinetmaker with a personal worth of $1,800. Cabinetmakers often doubled as coffin makers.

In 1834, Jacob Searly gave over his duties as trustee to Joseph R. Rudolph. Rudolph would presumably be the fellow who is found as a neighbor to Stearly and Paul and who lived in the same Sixth Ward of the Northern Liberties. Rudolph was a cooper.

These trustees (Jacob Stearly, Joseph R. Paul, Anthony Shermer and, later, Joseph R. Rudolph) appeared to represent the group of individuals that oversaw the West Street Burial Ground from its inception in 1831 until 1851, when the Union Burial Ground Association held a meeting on May 21 of that year to determine if the members would convey the unoccupied ground in the burial ground to Joseph R. Dickson for him to continue the purposes of the burial ground. On the June 7, 1851, the trustees of the Union Burial Ground Association turned over the unoccupied portions to Dickson for $150 with the stipulation that the land would remain a burial ground.

By as late as February 1861, the West Street Burial Ground was still reporting burials to the City of Philadelphia, as directed by the registration law put into effect on July 1, 1860. Any burials at West Street prior to July 1860 may or may not have been reported.

Dickson appears to have died by 1868–69, and a fellow named Magargee handled his estate. Vienna (Berks) Street was widened slightly in the year 1868 or 1869, and Magargee received $700 for damages to the property, which lost 27 burial lots due to the street widening. At this time (1868–69), the cemetery was stated to have had a total of 299 burial lots. Assuming at minimum of two to four graves per burial plot, the cemetery could have possibly held 600 to 1,200 graves but more likely held many more.

There would appear to have been a number of veterans of the Civil War buried at the West Street Burial Ground, as there is mention of the GAR's Walter S. Newhall Post No. 7 coming to the cemetery during its annual parade marches for fallen soldiers. The group stopped at the local cemeteries to pay respects to the veterans who were buried there. One newspaper notice of June 1, 1874, called the cemetery the "Belgrade Street Cemetery." By 1874, West Street had become Belgrade Street. It stated that the "graves of the soldiers and sailors buried therein were decorated, and Reverend Mr. Rexlaw, of Hancock Street ME Church, delivered an address."

According to Dr. Anthony Waskie of Temple University, George Leisenring, the first volunteer from Pennsylvania (Philadelphia's Fishtown) to be killed in the Civil War, is buried at the German Union Burial Ground of the Northern Liberties and Kensington. He was killed at Baltimore when a mob attacked his ill-equipped and mostly un-uniformed Second Regiment "Washington Guards," when it was en route from Philadelphia to Washington. The German Union Burial Ground of the Northern Liberties and Kensington is yet another name for the West Street Burial Ground.

The Decline and Closing of West Street Burial Ground

By the late 1870s, the West Street Burial Ground appears to have started to fall into decline. While veteran's parades may have still marched to the cemetery, neighbors were beginning to complain about the place, and the actual ownership started to be doubted. The city's board of health declared the cemetery a nuisance in 1876. Curbing and piping taxes were due. There was no fence around the cemetery, and there were even cases of families removing the remains of loved ones and not filling the graves back in.

At a meeting of lot holders in December 1877, a committee was formed to try and deal with some of the complaints. Henry Baldt was elected president, W.H. Mershon secretary and W.W. Sedler (or Seder) treasurer. A list of lot holders was taken at that time.

The lot holders held another meeting the following month (January 1878) for the purposes of fencing in the cemetery and restoring it to decent condition. By the next month, enough money had been raised and a wooden plank fence had been erected, with other work apparently done as well. The lot holders hoped that the fence would stop the encroachment on the grounds; they also hoped that the repairs they had made would remove the nuisance order placed on them by the board of health.

Apparently, the cosmetic repairs that were made to the cemetery had no effect, as by August 1878 the neighbors living along Vienna (Berks) Street across from the cemetery were back to complaining to the city. The cemetery sat about four feet above grade, and it seemed that "foul oozings from the ground pour out upon the pavement," creating "an intolerable stench" that was "compelling the people to abandon their properties." Those who still resided across from the cemetery kept their windows closed.

The cemetery complaints were stuck in the red tape of the city's bureaucracy, with the complaint being "tossed from the Board of Health to Councils, from Councils to the Highway Department, from the Highway Department to the City Solicitor" and then back to the Board of Health again. No relief for the neighbors was secured. After more time being tossed about in various departments of the city government, the cemetery was finally declared a nuisance by the city, and by mid- to late 1879, people were asked to remove the remains of their loved ones.

In January 1880 there was a report of a fellow being charged with stealing gravestones. On October 18, 1882, the *North American* reported that some of the graves in the cemetery were "nearly open, and disease is feared." In June 1884, an order by the city was passed to again widen Vienna Street, this time by a substantial amount. However, no owners were found for the lots that would be affected. The *North American* again, this time on October 23, 1884, gave a report of the cemetery:

DESERTED GRAVES
OWNERS OF THE LOTS OF AN OLD CEMETERY WANTED

Application was made to councils early in the present year to have Vienna Street opened, between Gaul and Belgrade streets, but when the matter was placed in the hands of the district committee of the Committee on Highways, it was found that no owners could be found for that portion of the old cemetery located at Vienna and Gaul streets, which was chartered under the name of The Union Burial Ground Association. Property owners on the line of the street were anxious to have the highway opened and graded, and eventually entered bonds to indemnify the city against damage. The ordinance authorizing the street to be opened was passed June 17, 1884, and as no owners could be found on whom the ordinary notice could be served, the matter was taken into court, and an order was obtained directing the Chief Commissioner of Highways to advertise for the owners of the lots on the line of the street, and if no one presented a claim within three months from the date of the notice, the work should be done as if the usual notice had been served. The time allowed by the court will expire on the 17th of January next, after which proposals will be asked for the work. Persons living near the grounds assert that no internments have been made in the grounds for years, and there are no marks to indicate that there are any bodies on the line of the street. If any should be found, however, when the work is being done, they will be reinterred in other portions of the ground.

The city still could not find any trustees for the cemetery. A search for Mr. Magargee, who had been handling Joseph Dickson's estate, the last owner of the cemetery, was not successful either. He apparently had died or moved away, and no other Dickson family member was found by the city. A court order was then obtained by the city, and work was commenced by the end of October 1884, with the order that any bodies found would be removed to other parts of the cemetery. However, this order was not fully carried out, as noted by this newspaper article taken from the *Evening Herald* of Friday, August 15, 1890:

BONES IN THE DIRT
RESIDENTS OF ALLEGHENY AVENUE OBJECT TO A GRAVEYARD BEFORE THEIR DOORS

Sergeant Reed, of the police station at Belgrade and Clearfield streets, was notified, on Tuesday night by residents of Allegheny avenue, In the vicinity of the Aramingo Canal, that during the day carters had been dumping dirt along the marshy flats on the canal bank at Allegheny avenue, and that among the dirt had been found human skulls, ribs, arm and leg bones. The carters had told some of the people who made inquiries about the stuff that they were hauling it from the site of the abandoned Union Burying Ground at Vienna and Belgrade streets.

Sergeant Reed, after gazing on the skulls and piles of bones for himself yesterday morning, reported the discovery to Police Captain Quirk, who said it was a case that should be reported to the Board of Health. As the cemetery is located in the Eighteenth Ward, in Lieutenant Tuttle's district, Captain Quirk and Sergeant Reed interviewed him about the bones at roll call at City Hall. Lieutenant Tuttle informed them that the work of removing the soil from around the old burying ground was being done by the Highway Bureau. The fence that once surrounded the grounds on Belgrade, Vienna and Gaul streets and towards the Montgomery avenue end had long ago disappeared. The grounds are higher than the sidewalk on Belgrade street. There are no walks on Gaul street or Vienna street. Between the western end of the yard and Montgomery avenue a row of dwellings has bean built on the old Gaul estate, and on Montgomery avenue, running up to the old malt house. There are houses on the upper side of Gaul street, opposite the cemetery, and on Vienna and Belgrade streets. The residents thereabouts have been complaining for years that the mud from the banks of the graveyard washed down and constituted a nuisance, and that the upper side of Vienna street had no footway. There appeared to be none of the Trustees of the old Union Burial Company alive who would redress the matter. The Highway Bureau had finally stepped in and was about to lay footways on Vienna street, where there never had been any and to replace the one on Belgrade street. To do this it was necessary to cut down considerable earth on Vienna street and as the bodies had been piled on top of one another in the graves in the process of interment, and all recollection or their identity had been lost long ago, the only thing left to do was to haul away dirt and all.

This article does not shed a very pleasant thought on the bones of one's ancestors being used as landfill.

By November 1885, a *Philadelphia Inquirer* newspaper reporter was comparing West Street Burial Ground to "Tom-all-alone's," the dilapidated street in Dicken's *Bleak House*, in which Dickens creates a powerful picture of the squalid environments of a particular piece of London. A neighbor of the cemetery, who talked with the reporter in 1885, stated that many of the lots in the cemetery had lapsed to the city, as there was no one left to claim them. She stated that the cemetery did not belong to a church, and thus when folks died off, there was no one to care for the burial ground. The article stated that an undertaker who used to bury the poor for free owned part of the ground and that he still owned it. This was probably George Thumlert, as Barker stated that he was the sexton and that the place had been called "Thumlert's" at times. Old man Thumlert died in 1908, and his estate was advertised as being probated in November of that year by his son, George W. Thumlert.

The neighbor who talked to the reporter remembered the last burial taking place ten years prior, which would have been the year 1875. It had been for a soldier. She may have confused that burial with the GAR procession that had taken place in 1874 that stopped at the cemetery to honor the soldiers buried there. She mentions the "high board fence" that was put up around the cemetery and went on to say, "[G]rass and flowers, of a summer morning it used to look real pretty." Unfortunately, the vandals in the neighborhood destroyed the place. The old neighbor had nothing but lament for the graveyard:

> [W]e have some powerful bad boys in this neighborhood. They got at the fence, and now, as you see, there's nothing left but the posts, and they have dug up most of them. They stood where you see those holes in the bank. Being higher than the street, the burying ground has washed down a good deal at the sides. Many people living about here have friends buried there, and would move them if the city would allow for them. Towards the last they got to burying anywhere and many bodies in a grave. One lady had a brother lying there. She went to his grave to have him taken up. They opened it and found not one coffin, but six. The lady said to put 'em all back again; she didn't know which coffin was her brother's, or whether he was there at all. Something ought to be done. It's a shame to leave the dead in such a place as that. You can see the boys are making a playground of it, and when pavements are put down on the east and west side of it the earth will

have to be cut away, and that will cut through some graves. Them that left the place for a graveyard little thought it would come to this, and its present condition don't help to raise house rents round it. The people about here used to be afraid to pass it at night for fear of ghosts.

The reporter finished his story on the cemetery with the following comments: "Thus spoke the resident, and in view of the neglect into which their long home had been suffered to fall, it did not seem wholly unreasonable to imagine it haunted, not by one ghost only, but by an entire indignation meeting of specters."

Because West Street Burial Ground was founded by folks outside of Kensington, and because its board of trustees members were from outside of Kensington, there was not the same connection by neighbors living near to the West Street Burial Ground as there had been between neighbors and Palmer Cemetery, which stood only a block away and was founded a hundred years before West Street. Palmer Cemetery is still intact today with a board of trustees that keeps up the cemetery and still buries neighbors in the old burial ground.

An article in the *Philadelphia Press* of March 13, 1892, stated that "the old Union ground at Vienna and Belgrade Streets is being torn out." The article went on to state that the ground was sold and that the remains in the cemetery were being removed to Northwood Cemetery. Northwood Cemetery is located at 15th and Haines Streets in Philadelphia. Today, a mass burial lot exists for those that were removed to Northwood from West Street. It is marked with a simple flat stone:

In This Plot
Repose the Remains
of the Persons Formerly Interred in the
Union Burial Ground
Kensington
Removed to Northwood
April, 1892.

It is said that there may have originally been upward of three thousand internments at West Street Burial Ground, but undoubtedly not nearly that many removals made it to Northwood.

Baist's Property Atlas of the City of Philadelphia, published in 1888, still shows the West Street Burial Ground as a lot, but it is not named. *Baist's Property Atlas of the City of Philadelphia* for 1895 shows two blocks of homes built

Two blocks of brick houses (today's 600 block of Miller Street), built on top of the West Street Burial Ground and Gaul's Malt House lot.

between Vienna (Berks) and Montgomery Streets and Gaul and Belgrade Streets, divided by Miller Street. This would narrow down the building of the homes on the old burial ground to between April 1892 and when *Baist's Property Atlas* was issued in 1895.

Prior to deciding what to do with the vacated West Street Burial Ground, the focus of the Philadelphia City Council talks began to be centered on removing the bodies and turning the old cemetery into a public park for the residents of the area. However, on December 16, 1891, Kensington lawyer Joseph L. Tull appeared before the city council's law committee and argued against the taking of the plot of ground at Vienna and Belgrade Streets for a public park. Tull wanted any new park to be located at the site of the Penn Treaty Monument (today's Penn Treaty Park).

Eventually, two blocks of homes were built on the old cemetery lot, with a small street (at first called Ridley, later changed to Miller) cutting through it. These houses faced Belgrade, Miller and Gaul Streets. No homes were built facing Vienna (Berks) Street. In all, about forty homes, mainly two- or three-story brick structures, were built to sit on top of the old West Street Burial Ground.

Much later, on March 14, 1936, a fellow by the name of J.E. Sturgis Nagle was interviewed and stated that, "I have an aunt who is seventy years old, and she remembers when they removed the dead from an old burying ground which was back of a malt-house in Kensington. They dug up the bodies of soldiers, and the diggers gave the buttons from the uniforms to children." This statement is taken from Barker's book on Philadelphia cemeteries.

Chapter 9

Other Historic Cemeteries of Kensington and Fishtown

THE JEW'S BURYING GROUND AT KENSINGTON: CONGREGATION RODEPH SHALOM'S CEMETERY

Congregation Rodeph Shalom was founded in 1795. It is stated to be the first Ashkenazic congregation in the Western Hemisphere. Its early members had previously been associated with Congregation Mikveh Israel. Mikveh Israel was the first Jewish congregation in Philadelphia. Due to a number of individuals wanting to follow the German/Dutch order of prayer, there was secession; in 1812, a new congregation was formed out of Mikveh Israel and chartered by the Supreme Court of Pennsylvania as the "Hebrew German Society (Rodeph Shalom)."

For more than fifty years, the congregation's services were conducted at several rented locations in the Old City section of Philadelphia, as well as in the southern portion of Northern Liberties. It was not until 1847, when the congregation purchased a former church and renovated it, that Rodeph Shalom actually owned its own building. This synagogue was known as the Juliana (Randolph) Street Synagogue. Juliana Street ran from Vine to Willow Streets, between Fifth and Sixth Streets. The synagogue sat on the west side of Juliana, a couple of doors north of Wood Street.

When the synagogue first purchased a cemetery, the members chose a lot in Kensington in an area that at the time (circa 1801) was not very built up—the area would eventually attract many other cemeteries. The cemetery was located on Duke (Thompson) Street, between Dean (Day) and Crown (Crease) Streets. According to the International Jewish Cemetery Project, the ground was first purchased in 1801 and wasn't sold until 1889. It is stated by Charles R. Barker, the Philadelphia cemetery historian, that in 1888 it was said that there had not been any internments at this burial ground in many years. Scharf and Westcott's *History of Philadelphia* stated that "the congregation obtained a lot for a burial-ground on Frankford road. Through this ground Ellen Street was afterward laid out."

Barker disagreed with Scharf and Westcott on the reference. The Duke (Thompson) Street ground was not actually on Frankford Road but rather less than a half block from it, and Barker went on to state that there is no record that a road named Ellen Street ever ran through the "Jew's Burying Ground." Barker might have been looking at the wrong maps. By viewing John A. Paxton's map of 1810, you can see that Day Street, formerly known as Dean Street (Barker calls it Shackamaxon Street), was not cut out yet; thus, the lot of ground where the cemetery sat on Duke (Thompson) Street actually bordered Frankford Road where Shackamaxon comes in an at angle. Thus, Scharf and Westcott stating "Frankford Road" would be acceptable. Scharf and Westcott stating that "Ellen Street" was cut through was an error on their part. They should have stated that Dean (Day) Street was later cut through, unless Dean Street was previously known as Ellen and this never made it into the paper record.

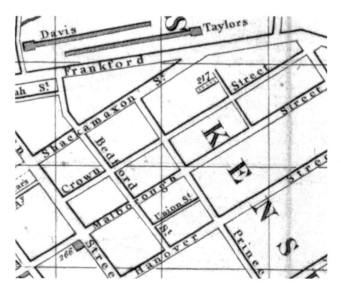

A snippet of the Paxton map of 1810, showing Congregation Rodeph Shalom's cemetery, called "Jew's Burying Ground," numbered 217 and located on Duke (Thompson) Street, off Frankford Road.

The Paxton map, published in 1810, distinctly shows the Jewish burial ground, listed as "No. 217." It is shown as a rectangular lot, with the short end of the rectangle located on the east side of Duke (Thompson) Street, situated at that time between Crown (Crease) and Shackamaxon Streets. Day Street was not cut through yet.

The Jew's Burying Ground is also shown on Carey and Lea's map of Philadelphia in 1824, Tanner's *Stranger's Guide* map of 1828 and 1830 and Carey and Hart's *Plan of Philadelphia* map in 1832 and *Picture of Philadelphia* map in 1835. Neither Smedley (1862), Hopkins (1874), Bromley (1887) nor Baist (1888) actually identify the Jew's Burying Ground; however, there are slight indications that it was still present on all of these maps, with either hash marks on shaded areas (Smedley) or with empty lots (Hopkins, Bromley and Baist). By the publication of the *Bromley Atlas of 1895*, the lot had finally been developed, and two brick row homes were built on top of it.

Again, according to Barker, the Philadelphia Board of Health registers show burials at this cemetery between 1807 and 1824. The cemetery is called by various names. It is called "Jews, Kensington" as early as 1823. It is also seen as "German Hebrew Ground" in 1831 and 1838–39; in 1859,

The Jew's Burying Ground site today, a block of houses on the east side of Thompson Street, between Day and Crease Streets.

there are references to "Rodeph Scholem," "Juliana Street Synagogue" and "Hebrew Cong. F. Road."

According to the International Association of Jewish Genealogical Societies website for the International Jewish Cemetery Project, Rodeph Shalom Cemetery (aka Rodef Shalom) had three separate cemetery locations: the one in Kensington on Duke Street and two others in Nicetown and Harrowgate (Erie and Kensington Avenues). Removals from these cemeteries were taken to Roosevelt Memorial Park's Section L. However, it is not clear if the Duke Street cemetery's remains were part of these removals, as it does not specifically state this.

The Philadelphia Jewish Archive Center (PJAC) is supposed to have some records for the Congregation Rodeph Shalom Cemetery; however, when trying to gain access to these records, I was not able to get a clear answer if the archive indeed had these records or not. The Jewish Cemetery Project states that the history of Rodeph Shalom and its records are described in PJAC's newsletters (no. 32, fall 1991; no 33, spring 1992; and no. 40, fall 1995), however, when trying to access these newsletters, this author hit another dead end with PJAC—the items were at a "remote location," and the archivist stated that it would take weeks to view PJAC's own newsletter.

KENSINGTON ME CHURCH ORIGINAL CHURCHYARD

According to the *Annals of the Kensington Methodist Episcopal Church* by Reverend W. Swindells, published in 1893, Kensington ME Church acquired a lot at the northeast corner of Richmond and Marlborough Streets in 1805 that measured 60 feet by 120 feet. The rear part of the lot was to be set aside as a burial ground and remained so until the erection of the present church.

From a trustees meeting of February 1, 1809, Mathias Wirts and George C. Schievley became the first committee to issue orders to applicants for internments. The price of breaking ground for adult persons who were members of the church was $2.00. For members' children under the age of ten, it was $1.00. If you were not a member of the church, it was $3.00 for an adult and $1.50 for children. The cost of burials for nonmembers was raised at the next trustees meeting on April 10, 1810. The price rose to $5.00 for nonmember adult and $3.00 for nonmember child. The sexton was put in charge of digging the graves. He was to receive $1.50 for digging the grave of an adult and $1.00 for the grave of a child. For serving funeral invitations, the sexton received $1.00 for an adult and $0.50 for a child.

The burial ground was located on the river side of the church, perhaps somewhere in the neighborhood of being eighty-three feet, six inches along Marlborough from Richmond, with a depth of about sixty feet. There would have been an alley between the church and the adjoining property on Richmond Street of about thirteen feet, six inches.

Swindell went on to state in his history of the church that at a meeting on July 18, 1809, of the trustees of the Incorporated ME Church in Philadelphia, the committee appointed to confer with the Kensington Society (Kensington ME Church) reported that "members of St. George's Church shall be entitled to internments in the Kensington Church Burial-Ground, on the same terms as the members of Kensington Society."

On December 5, 1817, it is stated that William Clark, the treasurer of the church, collected monies for "funeral permits," which would seem to be for burials at the church burial ground. In September 1818, the trustees enclosed the church and cemetery with a fence.

In a trustees meeting on September 25, 1821, it was so ordered to have all trees on the church ground, including the burial ground, cut down and prepared for fuel for the use of the church.

Monies from burial grounds were regularly reported in the treasurer's reports between 1817 and 1826. Judging from the costs of burials (mentioned previously) and the money taken in by the church, it is probable that there were anywhere from 285 to 720 burials at the cemetery between 1817 and 1826, depending on if they were adults or children and whether they were from within or outside the church.

In 1824, Samuel S. Kennard was appointed pastor of Old Brick Church. There were 257 members at the time of his appointment. After one year, he helped the church to grow to 359 members. He was reappointed for another year in 1825 but left halfway through the year. He left the church with 64 members of the congregation and founded what would later become the Union Wesleyan Church, whose burial ground was part of Hanover Cemetery. A little while later, 18 other members of Kensington joined Kennard.

On September 27, 1825, at a board of trustees meeting of the church, trustee George C. Schively proposed that the church should buy a lot for a burial place, situated on Hanover (Columbia) Street between Duke (Thompson) and West (Belgrade) Streets. This would start the founding of Hanover Burial Ground. The history of that cemetery is taken up in a prior chapter of this book.

By March 27, 1826, income began to be recorded for funerals at the "new ground." Money was still coming in from the "old ground" as well. On March 27, 1828, it is recorded that $165 was taken in by the church in "funeral monies." There is no longer a designation of "old ground" or "new ground," so it is hard to tell if they were still burying people at the "old ground" at Marlborough and Richmond Streets or not.

The following year, on January 19, 1832, it was first reported in the trustees meeting minutes that there was a call for the building of a new church. The next year the church was enlarged, and the front of the church was changed to Richmond Street. This enlargement included the purchase of a twenty-foot lot on Richmond Street next to the church that contained a two-story brick home, which became a parsonage for the church.

The plan of the enlargement of the church required a committee to be formed to contact the known "persons who have friends interred in the burial ground to ascertain weather their will be any objections to building the house on the burial grounds." Of all the people they could ascertain had loved ones in the burial ground, there was only one objection. There is no mention of how this one objection was solved.

By early March 1832, the monies for the old and new burial grounds were reported together; thus, it is not possible to see how many burials actually took place at the older burial ground. It would probably be correct in stating that there were no more burials at the churchyard at this point and that all of the burials were now being moved to the Hanover Street Grounds. In April 1832, the committee members responsible for handling objections to extension of the church over the original burial ground reported that they had received further objections and needed to hear from the trustees regarding just what the plans were before they were to start digging the new foundations for the enlarged church.

On January 16, 1833, the trustees ordered sexton Samuel Bacon to get a permit from the board of health, if necessary, to remove the bodies from the churchyard of the original church. On January 29, 1833, the trustees read into the minutes the following statement: "Resolved that the building committee be authorized to place the bones that may be disturbed in digging the foundation [for the enlarged church] and that are not claimed by their friends, on the lot—belonging to the house in which the Preacher resides."

This lot was the house next to the church, which the church had recently acquired as a parsonage. At the next meeting, on February 27, 1833, it was resolved that "[t]he Building Committee be authorized to dig out for the basement story, take care of the bones of those who may be therein interred & also to dispose of the dirt to the best advantage."

The enlarging of the original church would have encroached on the burial ground, on top of some of the graves. To enlarge the church, the trustees had to purchase sixty feet of the back end of the lot of William Sutton, an adjacent property owner.

By the early 1850s, Old Brick Church was outgrowing its expanded church of 1833. On April 27, 1853, a contract was signed to build a new church, this one to be sixty-five feet wide on Richmond by ninety feet deep on Marlborough. The new church covered the site of the old church, the parsonage and part of the burial-ground.

In 1872–73, the Young Men's Christian Association, in collaboration with Old Brick Church, built the Young Men's Hall behind the church on Marlborough Street. This presumably would have been built on top of any of the remaining original burial ground of the church. Presumably the bodies, if removed, would have been taken to the church's lot at Hanover.

An entry for internments at Hanover Burial Ground by Kensington ME Church stated that on July 2, 1887, "bones from church cellar" were

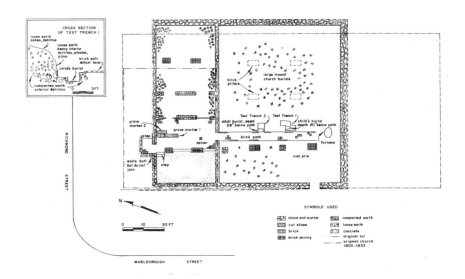

An archaeological diagram of Kensington ME's basement, showing where bodies from the old cemetery were found, taken from *Buried Past: An Archaeological History of Philadelphia* (1992).

reinterred at Hanover. This would have been from when there was some work being done on the church and bones were found from the original church's burial ground, now under part of the church.

Due to a legend that persisted in the neighborhood that Kensington ME Church was built on a Native American burial mound, Fred Pierce Corson, bishop of the United Methodist Church in the Philadelphia area, invited archaeology students from the University of Pennsylvania to come to the church basement and see if the legend had any merit. It didn't take long for Penn students to dispel the myth. They quickly found that the "Indian Mound" was nothing more than the work of lazy contractors piling earth they had excavated into the center of the basement instead of removing it. However, they did hit on a couple of graves and were able to determine what was already known by the church—that not all of the bodies from the old cemetery were removed. In an attempt to read the historical records of the church so that they could better understand the site, the students were denied access to the church records, a rather odd decision on the part of church officials since they were the ones who invited the archaeologists to study the site. This archaeological dig is written up in *The Buried Past: An Archaeological History of Philadelphia*, edited by John L. Cotter and published by the University of Pennsylvania in 1992.

FIRST PRESBYTERIAN CHURCH OF KENSINGTON'S ORIGINAL CHURCHYARD AND "NEW GROUND"

About 1812, a Welsh pastor by the name of Jenkins established Wednesday evening meetings at his home in Kensington. With the help of the Evangelical Society of Philadelphia, Sunday afternoon and evening services were also added. As the numbers grew, services were moved to Rice's schoolhouse on Queen (Richmond) Street. A lot was purchased on Palmer Street and a church built. The group was organized in March 1814 by the Presbytery of Philadelphia as the First Presbyterian Church of Kensington. The original church had a cemetery attached to it, as well as a schoolhouse. The present church, on Girard Avenue, above Columbia, is the congregation's second church. The second church was dedicated in 1859, shortly before the death of the church's longtime pastor, Reverend George Chandler, who was pastor of the church from 1815 to 1860.

The original church stood on the northeast side of Palmer Street, northwest of Queen (now Richmond) Street. The church purchased the ground from the Evangelical Society of Philadelphia. According to Charles R. Barker, the church grounds show up as early as 1824 on Carey and Lea's map of Philadelphia. Barker also states that the papers of the Philadelphia County Board of Health show internments between 1825 and 1829. It is unclear when the church removed these early remains from its burial ground, presuming it did at all. The members possibly removed the bodies from this early churchyard when they acquired their "new" cemetery in 1836 and deposited them there. It is unclear.

On September 2, 1815, it is mentioned that a school was to be built measuring thirty-three feet by eighteen feet and was to be built in brick. The following year, on August 12, 1816, a committee was formed to purchase the lot in front of the schoolhouse for use as a burial ground. By the next meeting, on September 10, it was reported that the lot for the burial ground had been purchased on a mortgage.

The sexton of the church was put in charge of digging the graves and caring for the new burial ground. In November 1816, Henry Moser was appointed the sexton. A relation of his, Jacob Moser, was a member of the board of trustees.

At a meeting in January 1817, it was announced that all members who belonged to First Presbyterian Church of Kensington could be buried in the church's graveyard for free. Those who were not members were to pay five dollars for breaking the ground. All those under the age of twelve were charged half price. At this same meeting, Jacob Moser and Christian Fans were ordered to procure a "bearer" for use of the graveyard.

On March 3, 1817, the rules of the graveyard were "published from the pulpit." John Evans was given the task of procuring a spade and hoe for the use of the graveyard. A gravedigger was to be hired. The graveyard was in business.

At the trustees meeting of January 1, 1819, it was stated that the president of the trustees was to be responsible for keeping track of internments at the cemetery and was the one responsible for giving all orders for the burial ground. This rule was amended on January 3, 1822, to allow the treasurer to have power with the president in overseeing the cemetery.

A fence was erected around the whole property, enclosing the school and graveyard. The fence and church were painted and the church whitewashed, giving an idea of what the church, school and cemetery area must have looked like.

John Myers appears to have been a longtime sexton of the church and the one who cared for the cemetery and managed it for the trustees. He was sexton for at least the years 1823 to 1835 and possibly longer. There is a man with the same name of John Myers who worked for many years as the gravedigger at Palmer Cemetery. It's possible that he is the same man.

On January 24, 1824, there was the first actual mention of the treasury receiving monies from the burial ground. There very well might have been burials earlier, but this first report of 1824 and the board of health's first report of internment at this cemetery in 1824 lead one to believe that this might have been the first year of operation or at least the first year that there was need for a burial.

It does not appear that the internment register for this cemetery has survived. It was supposed to have been kept by the president of the trustees and, later, the sexton. While the number of bodies interred is not mentioned, the amount of money taken in lets us know the amount of activity at least in the cemetery. The church took in from burials an average of $32.54 per year between 1824 and 1835. While the costs for a burial are not listed, if they were similar to the nearby Kensington ME Church, this figure might represent between 192 and 384 burials, depending on if they were children or adults.

The churchyard cemetery was probably fairly small, as by September 11, 1826, at a meeting of the trustees, it was suggested that a committee be formed to approach the Kensington Burial Ground (Palmer Cemetery) to inquire about burial plots. Michael Day, Jacob Keen and William Howell were the members of that committee. There is not a committee report of what transpired in their conversation with John C. Browne, a trustee of Palmer Cemetery. No lots were ever purchased or given to the church.

On October 9, 1834, the trustees announced that no person would be allowed to be interred in the cemetery unless he, she or they were pew holders for three months, with a quarter of the rent paid. This is far different than the previous rules (any member of the church being allowed to be buried there and nonmembers paying five dollars). The churchyard was presumably shrinking due to the enlargement of the school and the proposed expansion of the church, which began to be carried out in 1836.

At the time of the increasing need for a cemetery, the church's pastor, Reverend George Chandler, wrote a letter to the board of trustees complaining about back wages due him. The letter, dated May 25, 1836, stated that he had not been paid at all for 1836 and was still due money from the previous year. The trustees, a little short in the treasury, decided to fix two problems at once. They would purchase a lot for a cemetery and sell lots

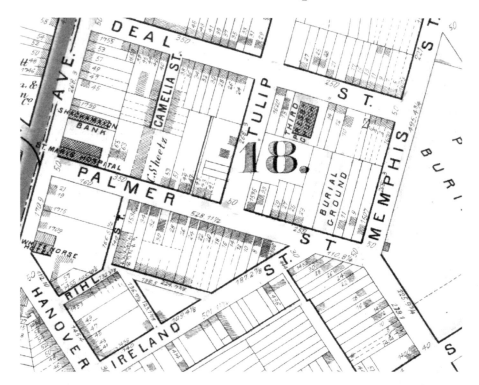

A snippet of the *Hopkins Atlas of 1875*, showing the new "Burial Ground" of First Presbyterian Kensington, located on north side of Palmer Street, seventy feet west of Memphis Street.

to raise money, not only to pay for the cemetery property but also to pay the back expenses due their pastor.

On July 15, 1836, First Presbyterian Church of Kensington purchased a lot to be used for burials on the northeast side of Orange (Palmer) Street, northwest of Lemon (Memphis) Street. At this point in time, Memphis Street was not cut through yet. The new cemetery lot had a frontage of 40 feet on Orange Street and a depth of 168 feet, 3 inches at right angles from Orange Street. The lot sat 70 feet west of Lemon (Memphis) Street, very near to Palmer Cemetery.

At the January 1837 trustees meeting, a report on the new burial ground was read. The committee, made up of William J. Seddinger, William Cramp and William Clothier, reported that they had sold twelve plots at $12.00 each ($144.00), twelve plots at $15.00 each ($180.00), nine plots at $18.00 each ($162.00) and one plot at $20.00, for a total of $506.00. There was only $46.00 still due on these lot purchases. There were also a number of single graves sold for a total of $96.50. Altogether, the burial lots brought in $556.50. The expenses involved in purchasing the cemetery ground, laying out the lots and selling them off amounted to $484.66, netting the church a profit of $71.84 in the first round of plot offerings, which was enough to pay off some of the money owed to their minister. Future revenue from the new burial ground would also help to build the church's treasury, but when the cemetery eventually stopped being an income earner, the trustees closed it.

With the new cemetery came some new rules. The sexton now—not the president of the trustees—was to keep a receipt book for internments at the cemetery. He was to present his report at the quarterly meetings of the trustees. Unfortunately, these receipt books did not survive; however, the treasurers' accounts did, and they generally show the name of the person who is being buried at this new cemetery. In the cases of children, it might only say the "child of" so and so. These treasurers' accounts are a good source of early burials for members of First Presbyterian Church of Kensington.

Money from the new cemetery kept coming in. The burial ground receipts for 1837 totaled $140.35. There was also a mention of $8.50 receipts from the "old cemetery," a sign that it was still being used (or perhaps monies were still owed on lots there). However, this would be the last mention of the old cemetery bringing in any money. In 1840, $122.55 was taken in by the church's new cemetery, and parchment was purchased to record the deeds to the plots the church was selling.

After about fifty years of owning the cemetery, and with the use of the cemetery declining, the trustees of the First Presbyterian Church of Kensington decided to close the cemetery and sell the lot. After proposing

The original site of First Presbyterian Kensington's burial ground, now a block of houses along the north side of Palmer Street, between Wildey and Richmond Streets.

the idea to the congregation, the trustees heard word from members on June 7, 1888, that there would be no objections to closing the cemetery.

On October 4, 1888, the Court of Common Pleas granted permission to the trustees to remove the bodies and sell the property. A committee was formed to oversee this project, and a meeting was called for November 1, 1888, to present the committee's report to the congregation.

At the November 1 meeting, the committee's report stated that it would cost $270 to remove the bodies to Northwood Cemetery (15th and Haines Streets, Philadelphia), which would include the new graves being dug and refilled and the headstones and footstones reset. The committee recommended Albert Emerick, superintendent of Palmer Cemetery, as the person who would oversee the removal aspects of the remains.

Emerick's cost would be $3.00 per day for raising bodies, and he would be able to furnish day labor at $1.50 per day. Yellow pine boxes, measuring twelve by twelve by thirty inches, could be made at $0.31 each to hold the reburied bodies (bones), and the boxes could be carted to Northwood Cemetery at $3.00 per load. It was also recommended that the new graves at Northwood should be enclosed with fencing of galvanized rails and marble posts. The fencing would be $118.94 for a total approximate cost of $600.00 for removing and reburying the bodies.

The committee's report was voted on immediately by the congregation and passed, authorizing the board of trustees to carry out the full committee report, which the committee did. On January 3, 1889, it was reported at the trustees meeting that the cemetery grounds was being sold to Henry Kellner. The amount the lot sold for was $3,333.33. At the treasurer's report given on May 2, 1889, the total cost of the removals and reburials came in at $823.11, about $200 more than originally estimated. The cost for pine boxes was $24.80.

With the cost of one box being $0.31, this would seem to indicate that a total of eighty boxes was purchased to rebury the remains of the bodies. The number of bodies removed could have been exactly eighty or it could have been many more, as the box's size would allow for the entire plot of bones (multiple bodies) to be moved together. It's possible that there were a total of eighty plots, and perhaps there was one box per plot. It is not known and may never be known, but there were eighty boxes used to move the remains of those buried at this cemetery.

Undoubtedly, like many cemetery removals, a number of bodies were left behind, and their bones sit under the parking lot that now occupies this site. The cost of labor involved in removing the bodies was $226.05, with Albert

The "new" burial ground site of First Presbyterian Kensington today, a parking lot on Palmer Street that serves the Memphis Flats complex, a new housing development.

Emerick charging $3.00 per day and offering day laborers at $1.50 a day. There is no mention how long it took.

The carting cost was $26.64, and at $3.00 per load, the carter would have had to have made at least eight or nine trips from Palmer Street to Northwood Cemetery. As might have been expected, "lawyer Tull" received $122.50 for his end, almost 15 percent of the total cost.

After the cemetery lot was sold and the expenses for the removal and reburial of the bodies paid, the cemetery committee was able to give the church's treasury a total of $2,539.09. Also about this time, it was reported at one of the trustees meetings that the church was going to undergo some needed repairs. The estimated costs for the repairs were in the neighborhood of $2,000.00. The gains of selling the cemetery were to pay for the church repairs.

Looking back over the trustees meetings for 1888 and 1889, the church's treasury was not that strong; in fact, it was overdrawn on a number of occasions. The needed repairs to the church and the overdrawn treasury makes one wonder if the church's reasons for selling the cemetery (reportedly because it "hadn't been used in forty years") were, in fact, accurate. A check of the treasurer's accounts show burials as late as 1867, or twenty years before they closed it and not forty as was reported. Perhaps the closure of the cemetery was more about what the burial ground was costing the church for its upkeep and how it was not bringing in the income it had in years past. By digging up the remains of loved ones and selling the cemetery property, the church netted more than $2,500, allowing it to repair the church and free itself of the problems of maintaining an old cemetery. Finances would seem to have been the reason for the church to close the cemetery, not usage issues.

Sydney's 1849 map of Philadelphia shows the original First Presbyterian Church located on the northeast side of Palmer Street, between Richmond Street and Girard Avenue (seen as Franklin Street). The church sat slightly back from Palmer Street, and there was some open space around the church, which was presumably the church's original burial ground. Smedley's *Atlas of the City of Philadelphia* (1862) still shows the original First Presbyterian Church lot located on the northeast side of Palmer Street, between Eyre and Girard. It also shows the church's new building on Girard Avenue. The *Hopkins Atlas of 1875* for Philadelphia shows First Presbyterian Church of Kensington's second cemetery listed simply as "Burial Ground," without a name.

Salem German Reformed Church's Jackson Street Burial Ground

The original burial ground for Salem German Reform Church was located on the west side of St. John (American) Street and north of Tammany (Buttonwood) Street. The ground was purchased in 1819 as a churchyard, with the cornerstone of the church laid that same year. This property was sold in 1876. The congregation had moved previously in 1873 to the former building of the Central Presbyterian Church in Northern Liberties, on the north side of Fairmount Avenue, between Third and Fourth Streets, the present-day St. Michael the Archangel Russian Orthodox Church.

Cemetery historian Charles R. Barker stated that a second lot was purchased by the church for a cemetery, this time in 1824, from the United High German Evangelical Reformed Congregation of the township of Northern Liberties (which had purchased it in 1818) "for the purpose of a burial place." The location of this burial ground was on a small street in Kensington called Jackson Street (later Ireland, still later Memphis), between Hanover (Columbia) and Palmer Streets. The lot the congregation purchased was the triangular piece of ground that sits between this stretch of Memphis Street and Palmer Park. The only stipulation on this transferring of the burial ground was that Salem Reformed must use the ground as a cemetery and also must allow United High German members to be interred without a fee for opening the ground.

Salem German Reformed did not keep the cemetery long. In 1869, authority was granted by the legislature to remove the remains and reinter them "in Glenwood Cemetery or elsewhere." The church had purchased in

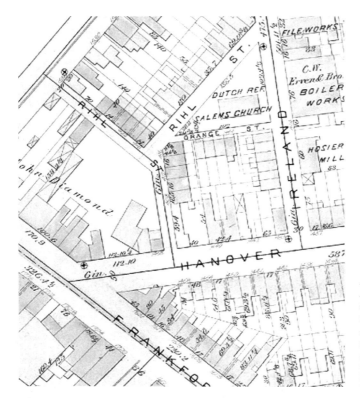

A snippet of the *Bromley Atlas of 1887*, showing "Dutch Ref. Salem's Church" on the Jackson Street Cemetery lot, the triangular lot between Rihl, Orange and Ireland Streets.

1853 a lot in Section M of Glenwood Cemetery, which presumably was the lot used for the Jackson Street Burial ground removals. Glenwood Cemetery was located at Twenty-seventh Street and Ridge Avenue. It was founded in 1850 and by 1923 had been taken over by the City of Philadelphia; the bodies were removed to Glenwood Memorial Gardens, at 2321 West Chester Pike in Broomall, Pennsylvania. As of 2008, Glenwood Memorial still had records of the removals from the old Glenwood Cemetery.

Papers of the Philadelphia County Board of Health mention burials at Jackson Street between 1826 and 1832. Its registers also show internments between 1838 and 1848. The registers also report burials for "German Ref. Salem (K)" for 1852–53 and "German Ref. Kensington" for 1853–55; occasionally the cemetery is mentioned as "German Ref. Jackson St." between the years of 1854 to 1858. Barker stated there was a slip of paper in the board of health's records that calls the cemetery "Salem church Burial Ground, Jackson Street, Kensington."

Other Historic Cemeteries of Kensington and Fishtown

Related to the Jackson Street Cemetery in Kensington, Barker stated that under the care of the Combined Sabbath-School Association (organized in 1818), a mission schoolhouse was established on ground a little north of Otter (Wildey) Street, where Hope Street is now located. The Philadelphia County Board of Health registers show burials at this location as early as 1819. The board's papers show burials for 1825–29, and its registers report burials for the "Combined Sabbath School Association" for 1838–39. The registers call the burial ground "N.L. German Ref." for burials in 1849–53.

In this mission schoolhouse in 1832 was organized the Second Presbyterian Church of Kensington. According to Presbyterian historian Kenneth A. Hammonds, the Second Presbytery of Philadelphia, organized by the General Assembly in 1832, received the West Kensington Presbyterian Church under its care in October, 1832, noting that it had been organized by the pastor of the First Presbyterian Church in Northern Liberties. This church was also known as Second Presbyterian Church of Kensington. The last reference that Hammond gave for this church in the Presbytery minutes

The Jackson Street Cemetery site today, replaced by a one-story commercial building, located opposite from the eastern side of Palmer Park.

was in a list of churches to be visited in 1835. After 1838, it was no longer reported on the roll of the Third Presbytery, and Hammond mentioned no record of its transfer, relocation, merger or dissolution.

However, Barker stated that in 1838 Second Presbyterian Church of Kensington was united with the German Reformed denomination (Salem German Reformed Church), giving his source as Thomas J. Shepherd's *History of First Presbyterian Church, Northern Liberties, Philadelphia*. The name "Combined Mission House" seems to have remained attached to the burial ground adjoining, which ultimately became a German Reformed ground. This "Combined Mission House" can be seen as early as 1824 on Tanner's map of Philadelphia.

Authority for the German Reform to sell this burial ground was granted by Acts of Assembly in 1853 and 1854, with the "bodies to be removed and re-interred within 60 days." The ground was sold in 1854, and the remains were removed to the previously mentioned Jackson Street Cemetery. An advertisement in the *Philadelphia Public Ledger* for November 21, 1853, posted the following notice:

> *The removal of the bodies from the burial ground, between Hope and Howard Streets, below Franklin* [Girard]*, will be continued to that of the German Reformed Congregation, on Jackson street, between Hanover and Palmer Streets, below Frankford road. Persons who are unwilling to have their relatives buried in said ground are requested to have them removed. By order of the Consistory. John Benfer, Secretary.*

Jackson Street became Ireland Street in 1858. In 1889, this portion of Ireland Street became Memphis Street from Palmer to Hanover (Columbia) Street.

MUTUAL BURIAL GROUND OF KENSINGTON, AKA HELVERSON'S

A surviving plot deed within the archive of the Kensington ME Church shows this cemetery to be officially called the "Mutual Burial Ground of Kensington" and stated that it was situated on the westerly side of Frankford Avenue. This deed, dated July 27, 1833, was made out by Jacob Coleman and James McCormick, acting on behalf of the cemetery, to a man by the name of John Clemens. The lot was stated to be "No. 89" marked in a plan or draft of the cemetery. Coleman is described as a "Dry Goods Merchant" and McCormick a "Boot & Shoe Maker." Both of the men were described as being "of the Northern Liberties, of the City of Philadelphia." As we saw previously, James McCormick was the president of Union Harmony Burial Company of Kensington, one of the three cemeteries that made up Hanover Street Burial Ground. Jacob Coleman was previously described as McCormick's attorney.

The cemetery plot deed described above stated that the "Grantee" who was purchasing the lot was to use the lot for burial purposes only and that no "person of colour or those who have been publicly executed" could be buried in the lot—this stipulation was the same for the three burial grounds at Hanover Street.

Sydney's *Map of the City of Philadelphia Together with All the Surrounding Districts*, published by Smith & Wistar in 1849, shows Mutual of Kensington listed simply as "Burying Ground." Sydney has Mutual taking up the entire block from Montgomery Street up to Norris Street and from the west side of Frankford Avenue back to Trenton Avenue. The Sydney map shows Trenton Avenue going farther south than it currently does. Instead of stopping at Norris, it goes down through to Cherry (Montgomery) Street to the old Kensington Depot. Sydney's map is the earliest reference to the Mutual Burial Ground of Kensington seen on a map. The cemetery also shows up on Scott's map of 1855 and the Lake & Beers map of 1860. Smedley's 1862 map, for some reason, calls it the "German Burial Ground," while the *Hopkins Atlas of 1875* calls the West Street Burial Ground, located near Mutual, the "German Burial Ground."

According to Charles R. Barker's "Register of the Burying Grounds of Philadelphia" (1943), the Philadelphia County Board of Health's registers have burials for Mutual of Kensington from 1838 to 1860. In 1859, there is reference to "Mutual, Frankford Road." In July 1846, there is one single report of twenty-three burials at "Helverson's," which had previously reported only occasionally. The report for Mutual of Kensington is missing for this same time period, which caused Barker to believe that Mutual of Kensington at this time was being called "Helverson's." Barker went on to state that a Mutual of Kensington report of 1832 was signed by "N. Helverson"—likely the undertaker Nicholas Helverson. The Helverson family also had interests in the Hanover Cemetery, having purchased numerous lots in the Union Harmony Burial Ground, which was a part of Hanover; Helverson possibly even took over Union Harmony completely at one point. The records are not clear. Helverson was the undertaker who removed the bodies from two-thirds of Hanover when it was closed in 1922 (Union Harmony and Union Wesleyan).

A death notice published in Philadelphia's *Public Ledger* of December 18, 1849, calls Mutual of Kensington "Helverson's Burial Ground, Frankford Road, above Harrison St., Kensington." Harrison Street is the old name for Palmer Street west of Frankford Avenue. The board of health has miscellaneous references to the cemetery as also being called "Mutual Family, Frankford Avenue below Norris Street."

While Sydney's map shows the cemetery running from Cherry (Montgomery) up to Norris, it is unclear just how big the cemetery actually was. This cemetery is sometimes seen as being listed at "Frankford Road

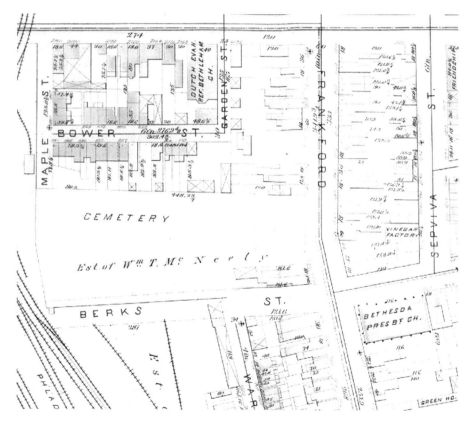

The *Hopkins Atlas of 1875*, showing Mutual Burial Ground of Kensington, labeled as "Cemetery—Est. of Wm. T. McNeely," on northwest corner of Frankford and Berks.

above Harrison," which would be "above" Palmer. The available maps, however, show that the cemetery was not actually located at the corner of Harrison (Palmer) and Frankford but rather was "above" Harrison or, as later maps mostly show, on the northwest corner of Berks Street and Frankford Avenue. It's possible that this cemetery was larger than how it appears on the later maps. However, after 1862 it appears to be consistently shown as being the lot on the northwest corner of Berks and Frankford that sat behind two corner houses at that location. Only two early maps show it as running south to Montgomery Street. Did Helverson buy up only one portion of the cemetery? Could he have bought only the northern section, with the southern portion being sold off? It's unclear. Further property research would need to be conducted.

G.H. Jones's *Atlas of Philadelphia* (1874), second volume, covering the Nineteenth Ward, shows a good outline of the cemetery and labels it simply as "cemetery." Below the cemetery, on the ground that had previously been shown as part of the cemetery, there is a lumberyard and "Young's Rope Walk." The cemetery sat three house lots south of the old Bower Mansion, a colonial mansion not taken down until the YMCA was built in the later part of the nineteenth century. There were two buildings at the northwest corner of Berks Street and Frankford Avenue. These buildings were three-story brick homes and not part of the cemetery. Behind these two homes was the cemetery. The cemetery was accessed via Berks Street.

The *Hopkins Atlas of 1875* for Philadelphia shows the Helverson's Cemetery lot as being part of the estate of W.T. McNeely. He owned the old cemetery lot, as well as the lot between Berks and Montgomery, on the west side of Blair Street (then known as Warder), running back to the railroad depot.

The cemetery was still shown on Baist's *Property Atlas of the City of Philadelphia*, published in 1888. It is shown as sitting back from Frankford Avenue, on the north side of Berks Street, with the Kensington Depot on the western border and some buildings along Bower Street on the northern border. A small street called Maple dead-ends into the northern border of the cemetery. This Maple Street was previously called Trenton Avenue before Trenton was shortened by the expansion of the Kensington Depot.

On the *Bromley Atlas of 1895* for Philadelphia, seven years after Baist's map, it shows an empty lot that was previously called a cemetery. Berks Street has now been vacated between today's Blair Street, at that time known as Warder, and the Kensington Depot lot. The *Bromley Atlas of 1901* still shows a blank lot, with no name or indication of what it is being used for. The 1904 *Atlas of the 18th, 19th & 31st Wards of the City of Philadelphia*, published by J.L. Smith, shows the lot now owned by Charles W. McNeeley, who also owned surrounding lots south of the old Mutual Kensington Burial Ground, on the west side of Blair Street running back to the railroad depot. The *Bromley Atlas of 1910* still shows it as empty space. By the time the *Bromley Atlas of 1922* was published, the old cemetery lot had been pulled together with the two other lots that Charles W. McNeeley owned and converted into the "Kensington Playground"—in my youth it was known as "Newt's Playground" after the coal yard that bordered it, but today it is known as the Shissler Recreation Center.

PEIFFER FAMILY GROUND, FRANKFORD ROAD, DISTRICT OF KENSINGTON

Charles R. Barker mentioned briefly a burial ground simply called "Peiffer." He stated the Philadelphia Board of Health's papers of 1825–26 reported "John Peiffer's" for burials of January and March 1825 and that the board's registers showed internments as early as 1822 in "John Peiffer's Ground, Frankford road, Kensington."

Where Peiffer's Ground on Frankford Road in Kensington was actually located is unclear. However, since so many cemeteries were located between Thompson and Norris Streets, it is probable that it might have been along there somewhere.

EMANUEL CHURCH GROUNDS

According to Charles R. Barker, Emanuel Church Grounds was located next to the church, with the church being at 1212 Marlborough Street. The Philadelphia Board of Health recorded burials between 1838 and 1860. The Historical Society of Pennsylvania has microfilm records of baptisms, marriages, confirmations and burials for the period of 1836 to 1919. It is unclear, though, when burials at the churchyard were discontinued or if the bodies were ever removed. Today the church has been turned into a private home; there is a garden to the east of the church building.

The First Presbyterian Church of Northern Liberties Cemetery

The First Presbyterian Church of Northern Liberties established a cemetery in Kensington on the northeast side of Shackamaxon Street, northwest of Bedford (Wildey) Street. The church itself was incorporated in 1813 and purchased ground for a cemetery in about 1818. In a book written by the church's pastor, Reverend Thomas James Shepherd (*The Days That Are Past*, Philadelphia, 1864), it is mentioned that one of the reasons the church fell

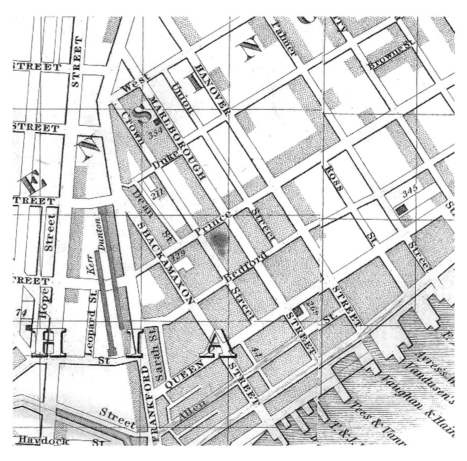

Tanner's map of 1828, showing the First Presbyterian Northern Liberties Cemetery (no. 129) and original churchyards for First Presbyterian Kensington (no. 345) and Kensington ME (no. 269).

The First Presbyterian Church of Northern Liberties Cemetery site today—on the northern side of Shackamaxon Street, east of Girard, a new housing development is being built.

into financial difficulties was that it purchased a burial lot on Shackamaxon Street in Kensington.

This cemetery shows up on the Carey and Lea's map of 1824. Tanner's *Stranger's Guide* of 1828 and 1830 indicate that it was "ground only." It also shows up on Carey and Hart's map of 1832. According to Charles R. Barker, the Philadelphia County Board of Health papers noted burials for 1828–32. It is unclear how long the church used this burial ground or what became of it.

Bibliography

UNPUBLISHED SOURCES FOR KENSINGTON BURIAL GROUND (PALMER CEMETERY)

Unless otherwise noted, following are in the possession of trustees of Palmer Cemetery.

Alexander Allaire and others to Jehu Eyre and others. Deed of trust for turning over Kensington Burial Ground to community, 1765. Xerox copy, original at the Historical Society of Pennsylvania.

Barker, Charles, Edwin S. Dunkerley and J.E. Sturgis Nagle. Tombstone inscriptions in Palmer Cemetery. Unpublished typewritten manuscript. Philadelphia, PA: Genealogical Society of Pennsylvania, 1953. Located at Historical Society of Pennsylvania.

Elm Tree Post No. 88 American Legion meeting minutes ledger, July 1, 1919–December 27, 1928.

Kensington Burial Ground interment registers, August 1, 1859–August 1, 1887; and August 14, 1887–June 6, 1980. Notebook of James D.B. Weiss, internments, March 7, 1976–May 23, 2007.

Kensington Burial Ground miscellaneous loose pieces of paper, correspondence, receipts for work performed or goods purchased for cemetery, small stack of internment permits (circa 1865), plus other paper ephemera.

Kensington Burial Ground treasurer's account ledgers, February 13, 1839–August 7, 1890; July 28, 1890–September 3, 1919; July 28, 1919–April 5, 1958.

Kensington Burial Ground trustees meeting minutes and treasurer's accounts, December 1765–November 12, 1838. Located at the German Society of Pennsylvania. Trustees meeting minutes, January 23, 1839–April 29, 1889; July 29, 1889–October 27, 1913.

Kensington Burial Ground vault registers. Albert Emerick Vault Book, August 6, 1871–January 25, 1874. A.J. Getz Vault Book, January 27, 1886–July 22, 1887.

Settlement of Anthony Palmer's estate, 8 pages. Xerox copy, original located in the Logan Papers at the Historical Society of Pennsylvania.

Superintendent's ledger for Kensington Burial Ground. Account ledger for internments, vault management and maintenance performed. Unbound signatures and loose leaves, 1873–87 (incomplete).

Treasurer's receipt book for Kensington Burial Ground, circa 1884–1913.

Unpublished Sources for Hanover Street Burial Ground

Following are in the possession of trustees of Kensington ME Church.

Correspondence archive of Reverend Garber of Kensington ME Church concerning closing and removal of Hanover Burial Ground; Brown & Williams, law firm hired by church to deal with city officials, including Forest Hills Cemetery and Mausoleum Park, proposals and contracts for receiving removal of remains, August 1921–May 1923.

Hanover Cemetery superintendent's register, Andrew Stoop, October 5, 1900–December 10, 1915. Includes notes on internments and vault usage only. The beginning period of this register, up to September 28, 1906, appears to have been perhaps a rewrite from the previous, earlier register of his brother Charles Stoop that he kept after he took over as superintendent from his brother. Andrew then decided to purchase a new register and record the total internments of his tenure as superintendent. The handwriting in this register matches the last six years of the preceding register.

Hanover Cemetery superintendent's register, Charles Stoop, May 1, 1882–September 28, 1906. Includes internments only. Some mention of plot purchases. The period from 1900 to 1906 appears to be in a different hand, probably that of Andrew Stoop, Charles Stoop's brother, who took over as superintendent of the cemetery after his brother passed.

Internment register of burial ground agents Samuel Adams, Henry B. Stoy, Joseph Bennett, February 1837–April 1, 1859. Includes names of internments and use of vault, plus monies paid for expenses of cemetery; there is some mention of plot purchases.

Internment register of burial ground agent Joseph Bennett, April 1, 1859–September 20, 1900. Includes names of internments and use of vault, plus monies paid for cemetery expenses.

Internment register of burial ground agent Elijah B. Goldsborough (for last part of register, unknown for beginning), October 30, 1900–December 11, 1915. Includes internments and use of vault, plus monies paid for expenses of cemetery; not as thorough at naming internments as the registers for 1837–1900.

Kensington Methodist Episcopal Church trustees meeting minutes, July 18, 1809–August 15, 1817; November 2, 1916–March 3, 1930.

Union Wesleyan Church Burial Ground tax register for plot owners, circa 1861–99.

OTHER UNPUBLISHED SOURCES

Barker, Charles R. "Register of the Burying Grounds of Philadelphia," 1943. Located at the Historical Society of Pennsylvania.

Helverson funeral records, 1841–95. Located at the Historical Society of Pennsylvania.

Remer, Rich. History of Union Wesleyan Church aka Pilgrim Congregational (typewritten), circa 1997. In possession of the author.

GOVERNMENT SOURCES

United States Federal Population Census, 1790–1930, as seen on www.ancestry.com, 2010.

PUBLISHED SOURCES

American Cemetery Magazine. "Neighborhood Committee Restores Ancient Philadelphia Cemetery" (July 1964).

Biddle, Alexander, ed. *Old Family Letters: Copied from the Originals for Alexander Biddle. Series A* with *Old Family Letters Relating to the Yellow Fever. Series A-B.* Two vols. Philadelphia, PA: Press of J.B. Lippincott Co., 1892. This was started as a series, but only two volumes were ever published.

John C. Browne and more. *Candid and Just Statement of the Proceedings Relative to the Kensington Burial Ground: Of its Actual Situation, and the Conduct of its Trustees.* Philadelphia, PA: self-published, 1817.

Carey, Mathew. *A Short Account of the Malignant Fever, Lately Prevalent in Philadelphia.* Philadelphia, PA: self-published, 1794.

[Chandler, George, Reverend]. *A Plain Statement of the Proceedings Respecting the Kensington Burying Ground for the Two Year and Half Last Past.* Philadelphia, PA: Conrad Zentler, 1817.

Cotter, John L., ed. *The Buried Past: An Archaeological History of Philadelphia.* Philadelphia: University of Pennsylvania, 1992.

Hammonds, Kenneth A. *Historical Directory of Presbyterian Churches and Presbyteries of Greater Philadelphia.* Philadelphia, PA: Presbyterian Historical Society, 1993.

La Roche, Rene. *Yellow Fever, Considered in its Historical, Pathological, Etiological, and Therapeutical Relations. Including a Sketch of the Disease as it has occurred in Philadelphia from 1699 to 1854.* 2 volumes. Philadelphia, PA: Blanchard and Lea, 1855.

Philadelphia City Directories, various publishers. Philadelphia, Pennsylvania, 1785–1936.

Scharf, J. Thomas, and Westcott, Thompson. *History of Philadelphia, 1609–1884.* 3 volumes. Philadelphia, PA: L.H. Everts & Co., 1884.

Shane, Dennis J. *The History of the Kensington Burial Ground Palmer Cemetery Founded 1732.* Philadelphia: Smith-Edwards-Dunlap, 1977. This pamphlet, apparently put together quickly for the Bicentennial celebration, is so riddled with mistakes for the history of the cemetery that it should be used with extreme caution, particularly for the list of famous people buried at the cemetery.

Shephard, Thomas James, Reverend. *History of First Presbyterian Church, Northern Liberties, Philadelphia.* Philadelphia, PA: printed for private distribution, 1882.

Swindells, W., Reverend. *Annals of the Kensington Methodist Episcopal Church.* Philadelphia, PA: self-published, 1893.

PHILADELPHIA NEWSPAPERS

American Daily Advertiser. August 24, 1822.

Evening Herald. August 15, 1890.

Fishtown Star. October 2, 2002.

Legal Intelligencer. April 21, 1921.

North American. October 18, 1882.

Penn Treaty Gazette. August 13, 1975; November 23, 1976.

Philadelphia Inquirer. July 19, 1848.

Philadelphia Press. March 13, 1892.

Public Ledger. December 18, 1849; April 21, 1921.

United States Gazette, September 8, 1803.

MAPS AND ATLASES

All of the maps and atlases listed here can be found in the "Map Room" at the Main Branch of the Philadelphia Free Library, 19th and Vine Streets, Philadelphia. Also, the majority of these maps are available online at the Greater Philadelphia GeoHistory Network, and most, if not all, are also located at the Historical Society of Pennsylvania, Philadelphia.

Baist, G. William. *Property Atlas of the City of Philadelphia*. Philadelphia, 1888.

Bromley, George. W., and Walter S. *Atlas of the City of Philadelphia, 18th, 19th and 31st Wards*. Philadelphia, 1887.

————. *Atlas of the City of Philadelphia*. Philadelphia, 1895

————. *Atlas of the City of Philadelphia*. Philadelphia, 1901.

————. *Atlas of the City of Philadelphia*. Philadelphia, 1910.

————. *Atlas of the City of Philadelphia*. Philadelphia, 1922.

Carey, E.L., and A. Hart. *Plan of Philadelphia*. Philadelphia, 1832.

Carey, H.C., and I. Lea. *Philadelphia in 1824*. Philadelphia, 1824.

G.H. Jones & Co. *Atlas of Philadelphia*, vol. 2, ward 19, 1874. Philadelphia, 1874.

Hopkins, G.M. *City Atlas of Philadelphia*, vol. 6, wards 2 through 20, 29 and 31, 1875. Philadelphia, 1875.

Paxton, John A. *New Plan of the City and its Environs*. Philadelphia, 1810.

Smedley, Samuel L. *Atlas of the City of Philadelphia*. Philadelphia, 1862.

Smith, J.L. *Atlas of the 18th, 19th and 31st Wards of the City of Philadelphia*, 1904. Philadelphia, 1904.

Sydney, J.C. *Map of the City of Philadelphia Together with All the Surrounding Districts*. Philadelphia, 1849.

Tanner, Henry S. *A Stranger's Guide to the Public Buildings, Places of Amusments, Streets, Lanes, Alleys, Roads, Avenues, Courts, Wharves of the City of Philadelphia and Adjoining Districts*. Philadelphia, 1828 and 1830.

WEBSITES

Family Search. Church of the Latter-Day Saints. www.familysearch.org. Includes Philadelphia City death certificates, 1803–1915, from several organizations located in Philadelphia.

Greater Philadelphia GeoHistory Network. www.philageohistory.org. A great website for Philadelphia maps and Philadelphia city directories.

International Jewish Cemetery Project. International Association of Jewish Genealogical Societies. http://www.iajgsjewishcemeteryproject.org.

Philadelphia Genealogy Research Services. Kenneth W. Milano. Encyclopaedia Kensingtoniana. www.kennethwmilano.com.

Workshop of the World—Philadelphia. Torben Jenk. www.workshopoftheworld.com.

About the Author

Kenneth W. Milano was born and raised in Kensington and still lives in that section of Philadelphia, where his mother's German ancestors first arrived from Unterleichtersbach, Bavaria, in the early 1840s.

He is a graduate of St. Anne's Grammar School, Northeast Catholic High School and Temple University. Before attending Temple University, Ken served a four-year apprenticeship as a marine painter at the old Philadelphia Naval Shipyard.

After college, Milano taught GED and ESL classes for eight years at Lutheran Settlement House in Kensington, where he met and married Dorina Lala, formerly of Fier, Albania. They have two boys, Francesco and Salvatore.

Ken also has a more than twenty-year history in the business of selling rare and scholarly books and manuscripts. He currently works with the bookselling firm of Michael Brown Rare Americana, LLC, of Philadelphia and received his training under Mr. George R. Allen of the legendary Philadelphia firm of William H. Allen, Booksellers.

In the mid-1990s, Mr. Milano, along with Rich Remer and Torben Jenk, helped to found the Kensington History Project, a community-based historical group that researches, lectures and publishes on the history of Kensington and Fishtown.

Visit us at
www.historypress.net